-THAT-
BOOK
FOR
Wives

SALLY POYZER

Ark House Press
PO Box 1722, Port Orchard, WA 98366 USA
PO Box 1321, Mona Vale NSW 1660 Australia
PO Box 318 334, West Harbour, Auckland 0661 New Zealand
arkhousepress.com

Cataloguing in Publication Data:
Title: That Book For Wives
ISBN: 9780995391727 (pbk.)
Subjects: Christian Living, Women
Other Authors/Contributors: Poyzer, Sally

Front cover Design: Jess Matthews, jessmatthewsdesign.com
Layout by initiateagency.com

Dedication

This book is dedicated to my gorgeous, patient, clever, funny, wonderful husband. I am so blessed to be your wife. I love and respect you deeply.

P.S. Thanks for coming up with the title!

 Contents

Before you start reading

Hi! Before you start reading you should know that this book is written for:

1. **Wives (or wives to be)**

   So many marriage books are written for both the husband and wife and explain how they can work together to improve their marriage. Women can find these books frustrating, especially if their husbands refuse to read them! So this book is just for you and only makes suggestions about what you can do, by yourself, to make your marriage a better one.

2. **Christian wives**

   I certainly hope wives who aren't Christians will find this book useful as well, but most of what I suggest is very difficult to do and requires God's help to give you His strength, patience, love and forgiveness.

3. **Wives who want a better marriage**

   Having a really good marriage requires really hard work! This book is written for women who are prepared to do what it takes to have a great marriage. If you want some advice on how to be a great wife, this book is for you.

4. **Wives with everyday challenges**

   Unfortunately, some women have husbands who are unfaithful, are addicts or are physically abusive. If this is you, some of my advice may still be helpful, but this book won't provide the level of support and answers you need. In this case, I strongly encourage you to seek the advice and support of your pastor.

So, with that being said, I guess it's time to hear how my story began...

How it all began

I was attracted to Josh the second I met him.

It was Friday, 1 November 1996, my last day of Year 12. I was sunburnt, smelt like pickle-juice[1] and was filling up a water pistol at our kitchen sink when he walked into my house in Mount Gambier, South Australia.

Josh had just arrived with his parents from Adelaide. His dad was speaking at my dad's church that weekend and at the last minute Josh had decided to come too. We'd barely finished introductions before he informed me that I shouldn't have left the dishcloth bunched up at the bottom of the sink. I wasn't about to let some stranger come into my home and tell me what to do, so I began to argue with him.

My mother shooed us and our argument into the lounge where we continued to talk until late that Friday night. On the Saturday night he said he'd come to youth group with me, but asked if we could have a Bible Study afterwards—just the two of us (sigh). That was certainly the ultimate pick up line for a Christian girl! It was great. We shared our favourite Scriptures with each other and talked and talked until 2.00am when my mum told us to stop talking and go to bed!

The next morning I talked with God about Josh. I knew there was something really special about him. It wasn't just that

---

1 Our last day of Year 12 was known as 'Muck-up Day'—a day when Year 12s would play practical jokes and have water fights throughout the school. Some of the kids decided to fill their water pistols with pickle juice from McDonalds, just to add to the fun.

he was tall, dark and handsome like I'd always dreamed, or that he was smart and funny. What really attracted me was that he genuinely loved God.

There was only one problem—while he'd been happy to talk with me for hours he'd shown no signs of being interested in me romantically. So when I prayed that morning, I asked God that if Josh felt anything for me, to please get him to say something before he left that night.

Sunday night, shortly before he was about to drive back to Adelaide, Josh and I talked for ages in the car. The short, unromantic summary is that by the end of the conversation we knew that we liked each other and Josh had told me that he hoped that I'd go ahead with my tentative decision to move to Adelaide in February to attend Bible College. As Josh and his parents drove out of the church car park, I turned to my youth leader and told her, "I'm gonna marry him!"

After five weeks of writing long, honest letters to each other, I met up with Josh in Adelaide for a day. That night he asked me out. He told me that he felt a call to full-time ministry one day and asked whether that was something that fit with my plans. When I said that it definitely was, Josh said that he wanted to make a commitment with me. I asked him to tell my parents that we were going out, so the next night Josh sat them down and *asked their permission* for us to go out. As a know-it-all 17 year old I was horrified—I didn't think it was their choice! Thankfully, my parents agreed. Later, of course, I realised that it was a very romantic and honourable thing to do and that having my parents' blessing was a great way to start our relationship, but at the time Josh's chivalry was lost on me. Shortly afterwards I moved to Adelaide to start Bible College and happily joined Josh's church and friendship group.

Seven months later, we broke up.

We'd been arguing about lots of little things and had decided that it wasn't worth it. Breaking up was devastating so we went to see our pastor right there and then, even though it was about nine o'clock at night. When we got there, instead of trying to prove our own rightness to our pastor, we ended up defending each other's actions and perspective. This made us realise that we really did love each other and that the little things we were arguing about didn't matter.

The next night, Josh proposed and I ecstatically accepted. Eleven months later we got married.

I was nineteen years old, enthusiastic and confident that we had a happy future ahead of us.

And we lived happily ever after, totally in love all the time, infatuated with each other and never saying a cross word.

THE END

Nice ending, huh?

It's fair to say it wasn't exactly that simple.

I soon realised that when you stick two very strong willed, imperfect people in a house together who have different personalities, goals and needs, that there are going to be lots of clashes, problems and differences of opinion.

In those first few years we had lots of fun, laughs and great experiences. We also had plenty of fights (Josh calls them 'arguments'), often over petty things.

When I was irritated, upset or angry with Josh, I would usually go to God and talk to Him about the situation. Actually, it was more like I'd go to God and yell, cry and carry on about how bad Josh was.

Most of the time, instead of agreeing with me, God would tell me that, really, I was the one in the wrong. Gradually, I started to see that many of the times I thought Josh was completely to blame, I was actually the one who had the bad attitude or behaviour, and that I was the cause of the problem, not him!

God began to show me that if I wanted change in my marriage, I was the one who had to start changing.

I fought against this at first, feeling like it wasn't fair that I did all the work. Fine, I could accept that I wasn't always handling things the best way and that I was often overreacting, but surely Josh needed to change too?

But God fairly bluntly put me in my place. He told me that there was no point waiting around for Josh to change before I would put effort in. I needed to let God help me change, and leave Josh to Him to sort out in His time.

I began to see that the success of my marriage was really in my hands. I could drift through my marriage, hoping that the good times would outweigh the bad, or I could step up and proactively work to make it a great marriage. I had the choice to make my marriage bad or good. I decided I wanted to do whatever it took to have a great marriage.

So I bought and read books on marriage and relationships, wanting to learn more about this business of being a wife. These books helped me understand more about myself and the way I interacted with Josh. I had so many 'light bulb' moments where the reasons for our differences became clearer. God also convicted me a lot through what I was reading in the Bible and my prayer times. I began implementing the lessons God was teaching me and saw almost immediate results. Josh was much happier and so was I.

I also talked with lots of other wives, who shared with me the frustrations, irritations and problems they were having with their selfish and inconsiderate husbands. I noticed that, essentially, all their stories were the same. The specific annoyances and hurts were different, but the root causes were the same. I shared with them the lessons God was teaching me and found that they worked for them too.

I began to write down these lessons on scraps of paper here and there so I wouldn't forget. As the years progressed I documented 50 different lessons, which later grew to become this book. When I sat back and looked at them all together I realised I could summarise all of them into one big idea:

I have the power to transform my marriage by choosing to meet my husband's needs.

This was big revelation. Everything I'd read, watched and heard was all about how couples could work through their issues together. But most of the wives I'd talked to had husbands who weren't interested in reading marriage books or going to marriage seminars. This just resulted in more frustration for the wives!

Instead, God had shown me that a wife has the power to change her marriage by herself, not by changing her husband, but by changing the way she treats him. If a wife chooses to focus on meeting her husband's needs, her husband is going to be so much happier. And the happier he is, the more likely he is to start meeting her needs, making her much happier. In other words, by choosing to meet her husband's needs a wife can dramatically improve her marriage.

This was great, but I still had a problem. My one big idea was covered in 50, yes, 50 lessons. How could anyone remember, let alone meet, that many needs?

I played around with grouping them for a while and then I had my breakthrough moment—I realised that really, those 50 lessons could be grouped into just four main needs. Not 50, just four. That's when I got excited, because even though a husband's main needs may not be easy to meet, at least they're easy to remember!

So, do you want to know what I discovered? What a husband's—actually, what *your* husband's—four greatest needs are? Well, here they are...

Every husband needs his wife to:

ACCEPT him (not **correct** him)

RESPECT him (not **direct** him)

CONNECT with him (not **neglect** him)

HAVE SEX with him (not **reject** him)

This book is broken into four sections, one for each main need. Each section begins with some Scriptures and ends with a summary of the key principles to put into place if you want to meet that need.

I want to warn you that that none of what I suggest in this book will be easy. It will be hard work and at times you'll wonder if it's all worth it. Hopefully in those times you'll remember that you are investing into the health and wellbeing of your marriage—short term pain for long term gain!

I want to be clear that I am not guaranteeing that if you do everything in this book that your husband will change. However, if you genuinely seek God's help to implement these principles, I can guarantee that *you* will change. The more you learn to be obedient to God and rely on Him, the more you will grow and the greater peace you will have inside.

I also want to point out that while this book is made up of things that God has taught me, I am by no means the perfect wife. Just because I'm aware of what I should do doesn't mean I find it easy to do! I am constantly working at this and often have to go back to God to ask again for His forgiveness and His help to be a better wife. So please don't read this book thinking that I'm some amazing, awesome woman who successfully does this all the time! I am still very much a work in progress. But I do want to give you hope that the more you seek God's help to meet your husband's needs, the better your marriage will become. This has certainly been true for me. We've been married for 18 years now, and our marriage is so, so much better now than it was when we first got married. Every aspect of our marriage is more enjoyable, more fun and more rewarding. The more I focus on meeting my husband's needs the more I respect and love him and the more I enjoy our marriage.

Finally, I want to encourage you to read this book with an open mind and heart. I know that a lot of what I have written can be confronting to women (as I've discovered when sharing these things with women face to face!). However, I hope that you will not dismiss anything you read in this book without praying first. Please ask God to give you wisdom and show you the truth. I'm still learning so my advice certainly won't be perfect, but God can always teach you what is right, good and true if you ask Him. And as the Bible says, *"...the truth will set you free"* (John 8:32, NIV).

ACCEPT

(not correct)

Colossians 3:12-15

Since God chose you to be the holy people he loves, you must clothe yourselves with tenderhearted mercy, kindness, humility, gentleness, and patience. Make allowance for each other's faults, and forgive anyone who offends you. Remember, the Lord forgave you, so you must forgive others. Above all, clothe yourselves with love, which binds us all together in perfect harmony. And let the peace that comes from Christ rule in your hearts. For as members of one body you are called to live in peace. And always be thankful.

1 Peter 4:8

Most important of all, continue to show deep love for each other, for love covers a multitude of sins.

Romans 15:5-7

May God, who gives this patience and encouragement, help you live in complete harmony with each other, as is fitting for followers of Christ Jesus. Then all of you can join together with one voice, giving praise and glory to God, the Father of our Lord Jesus Christ. Therefore, accept each other just as Christ has accepted you so that God will be given glory.

Matthew 7:1-5

"Do not judge others, and you will not be judged. For you will be treated as you treat others. The standard you use in judging is the standard by which you will be judged. And why worry about a speck in your friend's eye when you have a log in your own? How can you think of saying to your friend, 'Let me help you get rid of that speck in your eye,' when you can't see past the log in your own eye? Hypocrite! First get rid of the log in your own eye; then you will see well enough to deal with the speck in your friend's eye."

Introduction

God designed marriage to be enjoyable, rewarding and pleasurable. Nobody gets married hoping their married life will be filled with arguments, criticism, pain and betrayal. But unfortunately, this is what a lot of marriages look like.

So what can you do if your husband is frustrating to live with? If he is inconsiderate, selfish, ungodly, angry, mean or sinful?

Well, as Christians we should get our advice from the Bible. Do you know how many Scriptures talk about how you can help your husband be a better husband?

None.

Not even one!

Not even one tiny teensy one.

God never tells us we should try to change our husband, no matter how bad he is.

Why?

Because we can't change him! Nobody can truly change someone else. The only person we can change is ourselves.

It took me a while to grasp this truth.

When I first met Josh I thought he was pretty wonderful, but I also thought there were just a few little things he could do to improve himself. You know those long honest letters I mentioned earlier that we wrote to each other in the five weeks after we met? Well, one of my letters included all my concerns about him and the things that I thought needed to change about him. Yes, that's right. I wasn't even going out with him and I was already trying to change him. My motivation was good: I wanted to help him be the best he could be!

Surprisingly, strangely, he didn't seem that keen on my help. He replied to my letter, responding well to my concerns and saying that he thought I was great...just as I was.

Ouch.

My desire to improve Josh didn't end when we got married. In fact, getting married just gave me more opportunities to observe his flaws and to gently and lovingly correct him. Incredibly, none of my kind suggestions, hints and corrections worked. In fact, I got quite the opposite response. When I kindly hinted that he sweep in the corners instead of just the middle of the room he didn't do a better job—he just stopped sweeping! When I gently suggested that he separate the whites from the darks when washing clothes—he just stopped washing the clothes! It seemed like any time I corrected him he just got worse at the task or stopped doing it altogether!

It didn't matter whether I nagged, discussed, argued, hinted or prayed. Nothing worked.

Then one day God pointed out something very important: Josh was not my child, my student or my employee. I was not his mother, his teacher or his boss. It was not my responsibility to 'fix' Josh—it was God's!

The Bible says:

> "And I am certain that God, who began the good work within you, will continue his work until it is finally finished on the day when Christ Jesus returns."
>
> **Philippians 1:6**

I realised that I couldn't fix Josh because that's God's job. And if even God isn't going to finish changing him until Jesus comes back, what hope did I have?

This was one of the biggest lessons I learnt in my marriage. Instead of trying in vain to fix Josh, I should have been focussing my energies on changing *me*. I couldn't change Josh, but, with God's help, I could change myself.

This lesson is foundational to this book. Everything I write in this book is about how *you* can change, because that's the only way you have the power to make your marriage better.

The Scriptures at the beginning of this section make it clear that we are to love, accept and make allowance for others. We are not to judge them, but focus on ourselves. This applies to marriage too.

Our husbands need us to **accept** them, just as they are, not **correct** them.

Not to try to fix them just a little bit. Not to get frustrated with them if and when they fail. Not to judge them for their mistakes.

But to love them. To make allowance for them. To accept them.

This section gives you some suggestions as to how you can do exactly that.

He won't meet your expectations

When a friend of mine had been married only a month she was awakened in the middle of the night when she heard a noise in their new house. She shook her husband and said, "There's a noise! Go have a look!"

His response? "You go look!"

She couldn't believe it. Her dad was the protective type and she'd always felt safe in the house with him. She had assumed that her husband would also do all the 'husbandly' things like check suspicious noises. She was disappointed to realise that her husband was not going to be like her dad.

And yet...if her husband had told her that he wanted her to be like his mother, she would have no doubt been horrified!

Unconsciously we all have expectations of what our husbands should do or be.

Unless we become aware of these expectations and consciously choose to let go of them, we are going to be continually disappointed. One of the greatest causes of frustration in marriage is when our husbands fail to meet our expectations.

These might be expectations in relation to:

- His work (e.g. what sort of job he should have, how much he should earn)

- His faith (e.g. how often he should attend church, how involved he should be, how often he should read his Bible, what he should teach his kids about God)

- His kids (e.g. how he should interact with them, his role in discipline, how much time he should spend with them)

- His health (e.g. what he eats, what exercise he should do)

- His leisure (e.g. how much TV he should/shouldn't watch, what hobbies he should have, who his friends should be)

- His house work (e.g. what jobs he should do around the house, how he should do them)

- His appearance (e.g. what sort of clothes he should wear, how he should cut his hair)

The problem with expectations is that they automatically set your husband up for failure. He's not going to meet all of your expectations all of the time. It's just not possible, especially when he probably isn't even aware of what most of them are!

Even if he does half of what you expect (e.g. dries the dishes, but doesn't put them away; or hangs out the clothes but doesn't shake them out first and space them neatly) you will be disappointed and even annoyed with him.

And even if he does fully meet one of your expectations, he will get no credit for it, because he is just doing what you expected of him. He will only get 'credit' if he goes above and beyond your expectation.

ACCEPT

In other words, if you have expectations of your husband you are going to go through your married life always disappointed and frustrated with him.

The solution? Start with no expectations, then whatever he does is a bonus! Whatever good he does you will appreciate, instead of focussing on what he didn't do.

You first of all need to work out what your expectations are. One way to do this is to write down a list of all the things that your father (or other male figures in your life) regularly did for you and your family. This might include: mowing the lawns, emptying the bins, providing financially, paying the bills, providing advice, doing your tax and killing spiders. These are not unreasonable expectations. But... you didn't marry your dad, you married your husband. And he is different from your dad!

Next you should go through each item on the list and say to yourself, "I cannot expect my husband to [insert task here] like my father did. If my husband does do it, it's a bonus". Any time this seems a bit much, spend a few moments writing down all the things his mother did for him. Then ask yourself how many of these things you willingly do for him!

It is hard letting go of expectations. And letting go will probably be a continual challenge as you discover new expectations or as old expectations resurface. However, you will find that you are calmer, less frustrated and more grateful when you can learn to expect nothing from your husband and just appreciate him for what he does do.

He can't meet your needs

I don't know where it came from, but the idea that your husband should be 'the one person who will always be there for you' is completely unrealistic.

The truth is that no-one will ever always be there for you: not your mum, dad, siblings, best friend or husband. Of course, all these people probably want to be there for you and no doubt often are, but it's physically and emotionally impossible for them to always be there.

Your husband might be away in a different city, he might be sick or he might be stressed himself. Your husband might be emotionally damaged through an abusive childhood or work really long or unusual hours. Your husband may not be a Christian. You might even outlive him. The point is, your husband won't always be there when you need him and even if he is physically 'there' he may not be able to give you the support you want.

Too often women lean on their husbands and expect them to meet all their needs. We need to accept that this is not what husbands were designed for.

Yes, God did design men and women for each other: for companionship, love, support and making babies. But He didn't design women to be completed by a man. Only God can complete us and meet all our needs. Even if your husband is always with you, is well and is happy, he is never going to be able to meet all of your emotional and spiritual needs.

ACCEPT

Only God can do this.

And God is always there.

He never leaves or forsakes His children (Hebrews 13:5). He comforts us and understands what we are going through. He always knows the right thing to tell us (for me this is usually either, "I love you Sally and I will get you through this," or, "Sally! Get over it!").

If we forget that God is the one who meets our needs, it can be too easy to expect our husband to do so and then get upset, frustrated and even angry when he does not. This is why we need to have a close relationship with God and to consciously choose to depend on God, not our husband, for all our needs. Then any time our husband does show us support or help us, it's just a nice extra!

Nagging won't work

Everyone hates a nag. Consider how you react when someone nags you about something. Maybe:

- All right, fine, whatever!
- It's so trivial! Why do you have to keep on going on about it?
- I heard you the first sixteen times! I'm not deaf!
- Get over it; it's not a big deal.

Your reaction probably is not:

- Thank you so much for reminding me. I shouldn't have forgotten.
- You are so right. Let me quickly fix that.

If we hate it, we shouldn't do it! Proverbs 21:19 says, "Better to live in a desert than with a quarrelsome and nagging wife" (NIV).

It took me a long time to realise that I was nagging Josh *a lot*. I would nag him about pretty much everything. He would rarely respond, so I would figure he either hadn't heard me or hadn't understood. Because surely if he had heard and understood he would have done what I wanted. Wouldn't he? So I would repeat it again. And again. And again.

It was a further source of frustration that he was not only doing something 'wrong' but that he wasn't fixing it when I instructed him otherwise!

ACCEPT

21

God convicted me about my nagging through the *Incident of the Shower Screen*. Josh and I once lived in a two-storey 'renovator's delight' and our shower screen was a little sensitive. It was one of those three-panel affairs in a horrible brown colour and if you pulled at it a little too hard or in the wrong direction, the middle panel would come off the runners and jam the door. I used to get really cranky at Josh because the door was often jammed after he'd finished using the shower and I'd have to fix it before I could get in the shower. I kept grumbling about it every time he did this, going on and on about how he needed to be more gentle with the door.

Around the same time Josh kept telling me that I should bring my handbag upstairs at night time, rather than leave it downstairs near the door. I thought this was a waste of time. It meant lugging my bag upstairs every night and then having to remember to bring it downstairs every morning. So I usually forgot to do it.

Then one day God made me realise that these were two very similar situations. Not bringing my handbag upstairs was as irritating to Josh as him jamming the shower screen was to me. Josh wasn't deliberately jamming the shower screen to annoy me—it just wasn't important to him—just as I wasn't forgetting my handbag to annoy him—it just wasn't important to me! Once I realised that, I stopped mentioning the shower screen and made a point of remembering to bring my handbag upstairs.

What also helped me to change was to understand why Josh wanted me to bring my handbag upstairs. He was concerned that if someone broke in (which wasn't that uncommon in the area we lived in), it would be very easy for them to steal my wallet, phone and car keys if they were right by the front door. So, I changed my behaviour and discovered that it really wasn't a big deal at all. And, remarkably, I found that I was coping with not making any more snide remarks about the shower screen and just patiently fixing it whenever it got jammed. I also tried to make a habit of thanking God for Josh, not whinging about him, whenever I had to fix it. I figured it was a good, daily reminder to pray for him!

Interestingly, a couple of months after I started bringing my handbag upstairs and thanking God for Josh when I fixed the shower screen, I realised that I hadn't had to fix a jammed shower screen in a really, really long time. I don't know if it was a conscious decision on Josh's part or whether God was trying to show me that trusting Him would work out for the best, but either way, we both ended up getting what we wanted and it wasn't through nagging!

So, I learnt my lesson. Nagging doesn't work.

Then I asked God how this applied to future annoyances. What could I do in future if there was something that was really bothering me? Fair enough that nagging was out, but did that mean I could never say *anything*?

I felt that God gave me an answer, which is the rule that I have given myself since then. My rule is this: if something really bothers me, I can tell Josh **once**. As I only get one good shot at this, when I tell him I should:

- Pick a good time to talk to him (that is, not when he's just come home from work, or when he's busy doing something else)
- Focus on the action and how it makes me feel (or why it bothers me)
- Say it pleasantly (not nastily or negatively)

- Keep it short (not give him a long lecture!)

For example:

> "Honey, would you mind putting your dirty clothes straight into the laundry basket? It would make my life so much easier. That way I don't have to try to work out which of your clothes are dirty."

This is much better than:

> "Argh! Seriously! Can you PLEASE put your clothes in the basket? How many times do I have to tell you? It drives me crazy that you can't do this! You're actually being really selfish and inconsiderate. It's like having an extra child in the house! Do you even care about how much work you're creating for me?"

...and so on and so forth every few days.

If there is no change, I can mention it or remind him **once more** after a reasonable amount of time such as two weeks, a month or even three or four months, depending on the situation. In the example I listed above, I would wait at least three or four months before mentioning it again.

If he still doesn't change, then I just need to get over it. Maybe I'm being too uptight, unreasonable or unfair. The best thing I can do is ask God to show me where I can possibly change and to give me strength to accept our differences. Perhaps this is even an opportunity for me to bless or help my husband (it's really not that hard to sort out his clothes and put away the clean ones!).

There have been times when I've followed this method and Josh hasn't changed. Not even a little! But the awesome thing is, my attitude has. I've accepted that these things (whatever they are) are not important to him and that all I can do is thank God for him (seriously, many of these things are so trivial) and just accept him as he is.

On the flip side, if your husband is nagging you, rather than thinking: "He should just get over it", I challenge you to do what you would like him to do if the situation was reversed...that is, you should try to change! I have a couple of suggestions about how to deal with this.

Firstly, you should ask him what particularly annoys him about your behaviour. This is important, because sometimes there may be an alternative solution you can come up with. I know this isn't a husband/wife example, but I remember as a teenager having arguments with my mum because she wanted me to use hankies and would never let me use tissues. I thought hankies were disgusting and it was definitely not a fashion statement to have a bulging hankie-pocket. I fought her on this for a while until I finally worked out why she didn't want me to use tissues. It was because too often one of us kids had left a tissue in a pocket and it had gone through the wash, leaving tiny tissue flecks on all the clothes that took ages to remove. Once I understood this I was able to suggest a solution: I could use tissues, as long as I never put one in my pocket. Mum agreed and we both got want we wanted. She was happy and I was happy!

Secondly, if you can't come up with an alternative solution, I encourage you to make it your personal mission to change. Decide that you want to change if it's going to make his life easier, better or less stressful. Develop good habits or rules that will help you change your behaviour.

Let me give you some examples.

Whenever I ironed in the evenings Josh would always ask me later that night, just when I was about to go to sleep, "Have you turned off the iron?" Of course, I would always be 'sure' that I had, but once he'd asked the question I would have this nagging doubt. And so, because I couldn't handle the thought of waking up to a burning house, I'd have to drag myself out of bed to check if I'd turned off that stupid iron. One day, God gave me the idea of unplugging the iron every time I finished using it. This way, I would have a physical memory of removing the plug (it is much harder to remember just flicking a switch). Since then, I have been able to answer "Yes" with absolute conviction. It's such a small change on my part, but it reduces Josh's (and my) stress considerably!

Josh grew up always being taught to turn off lights when he left a room. My dad tried to teach me that too, but I didn't want to listen! Josh often used to comment that I'd left lights and fans on, but I would shrug it off, because it wasn't important to me. One day, God helped me realise that even though it wasn't important to me, it was important to Josh and that by not listening to him I was 'telling' Josh that I didn't think what he thought was important. I can't say I'm perfect at this but now I genuinely make an effort to turn off lights and fans, not because I care about saving money and the environment (although, no doubt I should!) but because I care about making my husband happy.

It's his house too

Ah, this is an area I'm still working on and it is very much a part of the previous topic!

I do most of the inside house cleaning (Josh does most of the outdoor work) and because I'm a perfectionist, I get very precious about things like people taking shoes off when they come inside, especially when I've just spent an hour or more vacuuming and mopping.

It's hard for me because I notice all the little bits of grass or dirt that fall onto my nice clean floor. This was especially the case when I had a house with cream tiles! Unfortunately I think Josh genuinely doesn't notice. This kind of thing doesn't bother him[2].

I've tried nagging, gentle discussion and getting angry at him. None of these delightful methods have ever been effective. After working for hours in the garden, taking his shoes off is the last thing Josh is thinking about.

Ultimately I need to accept that I can never have a perfectly clean floor, *nor is it necessary to have one.* I really need to remember this. The world is not going to end if there is some dirt on my floor. Life will go on!

And more importantly, I need to accept that it's Josh's house too. What right do I have to tell him how he will live in his house?

I had to remember this a while ago when Josh found a tennis ball and was bowling it around the house. I caught

---

2 Of course, you may have the opposite situation where your husband is the tidy one and you are the messy one!

myself acting like a mother, saying, "Joshua! Not in the house!" If he wants to bowl the ball around inside, that's his choice. It's his house! And if he breaks something, so what? I'll get to buy something new! ☺

You can't make him love God

A lot of Christian women struggle with the fact that their Christian husbands seem less than enthusiastic about God. They get frustrated when they never see their husband open his Bible, let alone pray.

Their response is usually to start the nagging. Or the not-so-subtle hints. You know, like: "Wow, that Psalm I just finished reading is so good. What have you been reading lately?" or "Babe, you'd better get up now if you want a chance to pray before you go to work".

These 'hints' sound so silly written down and even sillier when they're said. Our husbands are not stupid. They will not read this as nice wifely encouragement, but as nagging.

Another form of nagging can be offering to pray out loud for your husband. Prayers like: "Oh, God, please make him love you, change his heart so he wants to pray to you every day". Especially 'effective' when you slip a line like that in when you've kindly offered to pray for his headache, in the hope that when he hears you praying he will be stirred to action!

Then there's the push for your husband to pray with you or read the Bible with you. Yes, this is a lovely and wonderful thing. If you have a husband who likes doing this with you, cherish it and make the most of it. However, many people don't like doing this. Many prefer their own 'quiet time'. The Bible doesn't say that praying with your husband is a necessity. It's nice if you have it, but it's not worth worrying about if you don't have it! Let him take the lead on this one, if he wants to do it, then enjoy it. If he doesn't, leave it alone.

ACCEPT

29

We can't make our husbands love God. Only God can do this. As much as we nag, beg, suggest or pray, it is only God who can change a person's heart.

When praying for your husband I think it's best to avoid praying things like "God, please change him" and "God, please make him love you more". Why? Well, firstly it's putting yourself above your husband spiritually. It can start to feed a superiority complex where you begin to believe that you are the *real* spiritual head of the home. This is not your place, nor should you want it. God makes it very clear in Ephesians 5:23 that this is the husband's role. Secondly, you can start to get resentful towards God and/or your husband if he doesn't change immediately.

Besides, how do you know that your husband isn't spending time with God? When I was working in Darwin I used to read my Bible on the bus. I would pray after my shower in the morning, usually before waking Josh up. Just because Josh didn't see me spend time with God didn't mean that I wasn't doing it! The Bible does say to pray in secret (Matthew 6:5-6) and usually people like to be alone when they are praying and don't like to talk about it, so just because you don't see it, that doesn't mean it's not happening.

So how can we encourage our husbands in the things of God? The Bible gives a wonderful promise:

> "In the same way, you wives must accept the authority of your husbands. Then even if some refuse to obey the Good News, your godly lives will speak to them without any words. They will be won over by observing your pure and reverent lives."
> **1 Peter 3:1-2**

Our husbands won't be won over through what we say (talk is cheap!), but through what we *do*. Nagging your husband to be godly will never work, but ensuring that *you* live a godly life will.

So my thoughts are this: yes, pray for your husband, but simply pray God's blessing and protection on him. Don't pray that God will change him or make him godlier—that's God's job to do that and He will do it in His time. You are much better off spending your time on *your* walk with God. Get into the habit of praying and reading your Bible every day. When you pray, ask God to change *you* and make *you* godlier. When you read your Bible ask God to convict *you* through what you read. The more you do this, the better wife you will be and the more you will please and inspire your husband.

In my early years of marriage I discovered this to be true. Whenever I nagged Josh about his relationship with God it used to discourage him more than anything. When I left him alone and instead focussed on *my* walk with God, not only would I grow in God, but he would too!

One walk is enough. It's unhelpful to try to manage our husband's walk with God too. We need to accept that God will change him and help him grow in His own time.

God is your best counsellor

There will be times when your husband will be annoying, frustrating, hurtful and wrong. When these times occur your natural reaction can be to nag him, ignore him or fight with him. What's worse is that wives then often complain, whinge, grumble and moan about their husbands to their mum, sister, best friend, co-workers and even strangers!

I want to encourage you instead to talk to God.

It is unhealthy to hold in your feelings of anger and frustration, but venting them to other people is usually a bad idea. God is the best person to vent to, *always*. Not only is He your ultimate counsellor, guide and friend, He also will forgive you for anything nasty you say and will never tell anyone else! He will also give you exactly the advice you need to hear to move forward.

By talking to God, I don't mean praying that God will 'fix' your husband. As I said earlier, all this does is cement in your mind how wrong he is and how right you are! Also, you might then blame God if your husband doesn't get 'fixed'.

Instead, I encourage you to follow these steps below, which will help you to forgive and accept your husband:

1. Find a private room where you can talk with God without being overheard. Make sure you shut the door.
2. Tell God how irritated, frustrated, angry and hurt you are. Cry, sob, scream, shout, yell, punch a cushion. Don't hold back. Tell God exactly how you are feeling until all your feelings have come out. God can handle it!

5. Ask God to help you to forgive your husband[3].

6. Ask God to help you to understand him and the reason why he hurt you.

7. Ask God to help you to accept your husband just the way he is, even if he never changes.

8. Thank God for your husband and for the good things that he does (list them).

9. Ask God to show you if there is anything that you are doing wrong in the situation, then repent if He shows you something (you can be sure that if you ask God, He *will* show you if there is anything!).

10. Pray God's blessing on your husband. For example, pray that his work will go well, that he will be blessed in his relationships with his family/friends/work colleagues and that he will feel God's blessing on him.

11. Ask God to show you how you have been annoying or frustrating your husband in a similar way so that you can begin to empathise with your husband[4] and change *your* behaviour.

12. Forgive your husband again.

13. Go to your husband and apologise to him for your fault (if any) in the situation[5].

By the time you get to the end of this list you'll have a totally different attitude! I can say this with confidence because this is the process I usually go through. Using God as my counsellor always changes my attitude and helps me to be able to genuinely forgive and accept Josh.

---

3 For more advice on how to forgive, see *Forgive even if he doesn't say sorry*.
4 For more on empathising, see *His shoes are different from yours*.
5 For more on apologising, see *Apologise well*.

I've included an example of how you can pray like this below:

God, I'm so angry with him right now. I can't believe he did nothing. It's my birthday! It's the least he can do to organise something for me. I shouldn't have to organise everything for my own birthday! He's so selfish and inconsiderate. He doesn't think about anyone but himself. How could he do this to me?!

Your rant continues until your emotions are spent.
Pause as God begins to gently remind you that you
need to forgive. Pause as you grapple with this.

God, I don't want to forgive him. He doesn't deserve it. Would he forgive me if I was inconsiderate to him? Why should I forgive him?!

Pause as God gently reminds you that
He forgave you when you didn't deserve it.

Oh God, please help me to forgive him. I do want to forgive him, I'm just so angry right now. I know I'm over-reacting but I'm just hurt. It really feels like he doesn't care or even love me. Please help me forgive him.

Please help me to understand him and how he thinks.

I guess it's possible that he didn't even realise that I'd like him to organise something for me. I know he doesn't like anything done for his birthday.

Please help me to accept him just as he is.

Thank you for giving me him as my husband. Thank you that I *have* a husband when so many women don't. Thank you that he is affectionate and kind and generous. Thank you that he works hard for our family and that he is always happy for me to buy whatever I want. Thank you that he is great with the kids and makes me laugh.

Please show me what I've done wrong in this situation.

Pause while you listen to God.

Oh God, please forgive me for getting so angry at him and saying that he was inconsiderate and selfish. He's not. He really isn't. He really just had no idea what I was expecting of him. Oh God, please forgive me for expecting him to organise my day—I hadn't even told him what I wanted. It was silly of me to think he'd just be able to read my mind. Please help me to change. Please help me to be clear in future and let him know what I'd appreciate. But even then please help me to not expect him to do the things I'd like. It's not fair for me to expect him to do these things.

Please bless my husband, Lord. Please bless him in his work, bless him in his health, bless him in his relationship with his parents, bless him with many friends, bless him in everything he does. Thank you for him God.

God, please show me where I've not met my husband's expectations in the past, where I've hurt his feelings by not considering what he wants.

Pause while you listen to God.

Oh God, I guess maybe I've done the opposite—in the past I've organised big birthday parties for my husband and invited everyone we know—and he really doesn't seem to like that. I thought he was just being difficult and anti-social, but really he's just different—maybe for him he prefers just having time with me and the kids on his birthday and maybe seeing his parents. Oh God, please forgive me for being inconsiderate and selfish—organising for him what I wanted for me, instead of asking him what he actually wanted.

Oh God, I do truly forgive him. He was doing for me what he would like: giving me a relaxing day, with no plans or stress. Please help me to explain to him how I'm different and be patient with him if he doesn't understand. I love him and appreciate him. Thank you God. Thank you for helping me understand myself and him better. Please help me to try to understand him in future instead of being so quick to get angry. Help me to believe the best of him, not the worst.

Of course this is a made up scenario and response, but I hope you can see from this example how if we take our problems to God, He can change our hearts and use a bad situation to help us grow in our character.

After going through this process, if the issue is so significant that you really feel you need to speak to someone, such as your pastor, I suggest you approach your husband very respectfully (after lots of prayer!) and say something like:

Honey, I really want to be the best wife I can be for you. I am struggling to do this in relation to [your issue]. I feel like I need some guidance as to how I can better handle this situation. Would you be supportive of either both of us, or just me, if you'd prefer, going to see my/our pastor so I can get some advice about how to handle this better?

Most men would rather get a bullet in their leg than get counselling. To talk about their feelings and their problems is highly embarrassing for them. Men don't usually like to get help, they like to figure things out on their own. If you approach your husband like this, though, you are giving him the option of coming or not. You are also respectfully involving him, which is much better than him finding out later that you've been talking about him behind his back. Also, you are being clear that your intention for getting counselling is not to whinge about him, but to gain advice for how you can better respond.

Your pastor should be able to provide you with godly, Biblically-based advice and pray with you (if they feel unequipped to counsel you, ask them to recommend a good Christian counsellor). Go to your pastor not to seek support for your 'side' of the issue, but to get tools for responding to your husband in a godly manner. Pray beforehand that God will give your pastor wisdom and afterwards pray that God shows you exactly what you need to do next. God has the answers you need. Keep asking and he will guide you.

His shoes are different from yours

As I mentioned in the previous topic, empathising can be very valuable. When Josh and I first got married I was really irritated because he always put music on. I grew up in a home where we never listened to the radio and usually the only music we listened to was church music. I am just not a music kind of person. I probably put music on for myself a couple of times a year and I always turn the radio off when I drive. So when Josh kept putting music on when we first got married I would get annoyed and ask him to turn it off, or at the very least turn it down. I thought it was very anti-social because it made it harder for us to talk and it distracted him if I was trying to tell him something.

I must have been praying about it because one day I suddenly realised that Josh listening to music was like me reading books. Early on in our marriage Josh had discovered that I loved reading. Whenever I had the chance I would read. I would have a couple of books on the go at any given time and as soon as I finished one I would get out another. Josh started to complain about how much I read, saying it was anti-social because I would never want to talk to him or listen to him when I was reading. I thought he was over-reacting and that he didn't understand how enjoyable and relaxing I found reading.

Realising that the way I felt about books was the same way he felt about music was massive. It showed me that he didn't turn music on to annoy me, but to relax and because he enjoyed it—just like I didn't read to annoy him, but to relax and because I enjoyed it.

This didn't make me like listening to music all of a sudden, but it did make me much more tolerant of it. I stopped complaining and accepted it. It also made me realise that I needed to cut down how much I read. A book should never be more important than talking with or spending time with my husband!

And in case you're wondering, many, many years of listening to Josh's music have increased my appreciation of music and, while I still don't listen to music when I'm by myself, I find that I enjoy his music (mostly) when he puts it on. I no longer have to make myself tolerate it!

He is different, not wrong

Your husband is so, so different from you. For example:

1. He's a man, not a woman

This may seem fairly obvious, but it's worth thinking about! God designed him completely different to you. His body is very clearly different from yours. God designed a man's body to be stronger and faster so he can provide for and protect his family. God designed a woman's body to be softer and curvier so she can have children and breastfeed. This is not sexist, this is just reality. This doesn't make men better than women or women better than men—it just makes us different!

And it's not just his body that's different—but also the way he thinks. A five minute video really worth watching is Mark Gungor's *Men's Brain Women's Brain*, which can easily be found online. Mark explains in a humorous way how men think about one topic at a time, while women can't do this because *everything* is connected. I know this is true! When talking with Josh I jump from topic to topic all the time—because one thought will trigger another thought which will remind me of something else...it's just the way I'm wired.

Another good resource which explores the difference between men and women is John Gray's best-selling book *Men Are from Mars, Women Are from Venus*[6]. While it isn't a Christian book and I don't agree with some of his approaches, his ways of explaining the

6 *Men are from Mars, Women are from Venus*, John Gray, 1992, Thorsons

differences between men and women can be very helpful.

Understanding that your husband is like other men can help you be more accepting of his differences. God has made him different from you for a reason. It's a good idea to ask God to help you understand why He has made your husband that way and to also show you how his masculine differences bring something positive to your relationship.

2. He has a different personality

Personality Plus by Florence Littauer[7] is another fantastic book that I recommend to everyone. Florence explains that there are four different personality types:

Sanguine
A Sanguine is the life of the party, an extrovert and very talkative. They usually have lots of friends.

Melancholy
A Melancholy is serious, sensitive, analytical, very organised and a perfectionist. They can be artistic or musical.

Choleric
A Choleric is a leader, strong willed, confident, independent and goal orientated.

Phlegmatic
A Phlegmatic is relaxed, easy going, pleasant, steady and good under pressure.

---

7 *Personality Plus*, Florence Littauer, 1983, Revell

This easy to read book is very useful for helping you understand your husband's personality, as well as your own. What I particularly like is Florence's practical suggestions for how to work on your own weaknesses and also how to work with your spouse's different personality. Buy it. Read it. Please. It's worth the small investment of your time and money.

3. He has a different love language to you

Another excellent book everyone should read is *The Five Love Languages* by Dr Gary Chapman[8]. Dr Gary explains that there are five main ways to give and receive love but that most people prefer to receive love in one or two of these ways. You'll probably be able to quickly identify which love language(s) you'd like your spouse to use to show you love:

Quality Time
Quality Time is about regularly talking and spending time together, giving the other person your undivided attention.

Words of Affirmation
Words of Affirmation is about telling the other person how much you love them, appreciate them, respect them, admire them, are attracted to them and so on.

Gifts
Gifts is not so much about the cost of the gift (it can be free!) it is more the idea that the other person was thinking about you and took the time to choose something meaningful to you.

8 *The Five Love Languages*, Gary Chapman, 1992, Strand Publishing

Acts of Service
Acts of Service is about doing things for the other person that they appreciate: housework, looking after the kids, filling the car with petrol, doing their tax, getting them a coffee, giving them a massage.

Physical Touch
Physical Touch is about connecting physically with the other person through holding hands, hugs, kisses or even just touching them on the arm as they walk past.

When you identify your love language it can help you understand why sometimes (or all the time!) you may feel that your husband doesn't love you.

Early on in our marriage I used to fairly regularly ask Josh (often with tears in my eyes): "Do you even love me?!?" Reading Dr Gray's book helped me understand that our love languages are completely different. I like all of the love languages (greedy, I know!) but to really feel loved I need *Physical Touch* and *Words of Affirmation* whereas Josh needs *Acts of Service*. Once I realised that this was Josh's love language, I was able to interpret all the things he did for me as love! I just thought he was doing them because they were his jobs, I didn't realise they were an expression of his love for me.

Discovering that *Physical Touch* was most definitely not his love language also helped me realise why he never wanted to hold my hand or put his arm around me in public. This is just so natural for me, but he finds this awkward and uncomfortable. In the early days I interpreted his lack of PDAs (Public Displays of Affection) as a lack of love, but now I know he is just not a 'touchy feely' person like me. I learnt to accept that he will always struggle to show love to me in the way I like. Given that nearly everyone marries someone who has a different love language to them, you may need to accept this too!

An even more important thing I learnt from this book was to *stop* trying to show love to Josh in the way *I* like and to *start* showing love to him in a way that *he* likes. I find this very difficult. It is so easy for me to touch Josh, hug him, kiss him, hold his hand and tell him how wonderful I think he is. It is so hard for me to take the effort to make him a cup of tea, pack him some lunch, iron his shirts or give him a massage. It's so time consuming and boring! God has really had to challenge me on this over the years. He's had to keep reminding me to invest the time and effort into my marriage by happily and willingly doing *Acts of Service* for my husband, in the same way that I'd love him to happily and willingly hug me and tell me he loves me.

God has also had to help me stop touching Josh all the time and telling him 20 times a day that I love him. It's not just that these things aren't his love language, they actually annoy him. We are so different in what we like and don't like!

4. He has different needs to you

Willard F. Harley's best-selling book *His Needs, Her Needs*[9] is another very worthwhile read. In his practice as a clinical psychologist and as a marriage therapist he discovered that most people's emotional needs in a marriage could be classified into one of ten different areas of need. Interestingly, when he asked married couples to rank these needs according to their priority,

9 *His Needs, Her Needs*, Willard Harley, 1986, Monarch Books

he usually found that the ones that the women listed as their top five, their husbands listed as their bottom five and vice versa! He also found that most women picked the same five and that most men picked the same five (the order may vary from person to person). He lists these needs as follows:

Top Five Needs for Women

1. Affection
2. Intimate Conversation
3. Honesty and Openness
4. Financial Support (enough money to live comfortably)
5. Family Commitment (be a good father)

Top Five Needs for Men

1. Sexual Fulfilment
2. Recreational Companionship
3. Physical Attractiveness
4. Domestic Support (peace and quiet)
5. Admiration (be proud of him)

It would be an interesting exercise for you to write these 10 needs down in a random order and ask your husband (if he's willing) to rank them in order of priority to him. You could then compare his rankings to how you would rank them. I think it would highlight that your husband's needs are very different from yours!

In summary: God made your husband a man (not a woman), he gave him a different personality, a different love language and different needs. In other words: your husband is different, not wrong! Some things that are really important to you he won't ever even notice. Some things that make you happy and excited will be boring to him. Some things that you desperately need he won't even want.

We need to accept that our husbands are men and will act like men, that they have a different personality to us, a different love language and different needs. When we can accept this, and accept our husbands for who they are (different from us, not wrong), it actually brings a huge amount of peace. We get less frustrated, less insecure, less irritated and less angry.

I know that has certainly been the case in my marriage. A lot of things that really upset me in the early days are now things that I can just shrug at. Those things really don't matter because now I am learning to understand and appreciate my husband for who he is, not who I thought he should be. It has really helped me relax and be less uptight. This makes me far more pleasant to be around which makes Josh happier. And when he's happier, he's even more loving to me. Win-win all around!

He will have his quirks

Everyone has their little quirks: things about them that are different from the norm. You have yours (which are perfectly justifiable, of course!) and he has his. Maybe he really doesn't like pineapple or is scared of heights. Perhaps he hates meeting new people or tells really dumb jokes.

Often we find these little quirks amusing and interesting when we're dating, but once we're married they can become irritating and frustrating, especially if they impact on our ability to do what we want! For example, it might mean you never get to order ham and pineapple pizza, or you can't climb the Sydney Harbour Bridge together. It might mean you rarely get to invite new couples over for dinner or you regularly get embarrassed when he tries to be funny.

Much worse: he will also have his areas of temptation to sin. We all have particular areas where we are weaker and where we are more likely to sin, for example, we might be tempted with arrogance, rudeness, selfishness, fear, jealousy, criticism, obsession or perfectionism. God can help us but we will always have to be aware of and cautious about these areas.

Whatever your husband's quirks or areas of temptation are, there's really nothing you can do about it. These things are unlikely to change. You are stuck with them for the rest of your lives together.

Instead of nagging him, getting frustrated with him or trying to force him to change, I suggest you ask God to help you accept him. That doesn't mean you approve of them or think they are good, it just means you recognise that your

ACCEPT

husband, just like you, has his quirks and temptations, and that your husband, just like you, needs God's grace and mercy. Remembering that you have your own quirks and temptations will help you do this.

It might also help to think about some of the 'worse' quirks and temptations out there and be grateful that at least your husband doesn't have those!

Being 'in love' is different from real love

There is a huge difference between being 'in love' and real love.

'In love' is a feeling love. It's warm fuzzies, butterflies in the stomach, sweaty palms and the roller-coaster of "Does he like me or doesn't he like me?" This is a great time in a relationship. It's exciting and scary because there is nothing definite. The possibilities are endless.

However, if a relationship continues and results in the commitment of marriage, the 'in love' feelings will very quickly disappear. This is normal and right. That is because the 'in love' feelings come from uncertainty, whereas marriage is all about certainty! You can't have both commitment love and 'in love' feelings at the same time.

But it is the commitment love that is far more valuable and more wonderful. This is the love that has demonstrated itself publicly in front of family and friends, that allows planning for the future and that endures through the bad times. It is good to enjoy the 'in love' feelings while they last, but it's also good to enjoy commitment love if you're blessed with it.

Unfortunately so many people think that the 'in love' feeling is what love is all about and leave a relationship as soon as the feeling starts to fade, moving from relationship to relationship in search of that feeling. This can often be the person who tells you they are looking for 'the one'. They allow a temporary good thing become the goal instead of a permanent great thing.

So don't be disheartened if you no longer have those 'in love' feelings that you had when you first met your husband. This is normal and right. Instead, be grateful that you have reached the better phase and do everything you can to show your husband real, lasting and satisfying commitment love.

Showing love is better than feeling love

I *feel* love a lot. I still look at Josh sometimes and sigh, wondering how I was so blessed to get such a good looking, funny and intelligent husband. I feel all warm and fuzzy when he holds my hand or gives me an unexpected hug. I get excited when he rings me for no reason except to say hello.

Unfortunately, Josh doesn't seem to feel the same way. Maybe he gazes at me when I'm sleeping (like I do to him)... but somehow I doubt it. He's just not that kind of guy. I used to really struggle with this and wonder whether he even loved me.

Then one day he tore a ligament in his ankle playing volleyball. I had to take a day off work, drive him around for a week, do all the housework and gardening and help him walk. It took weeks and weeks for him to get back to health. Very quickly I became impatient with him and got sick of having to look after him.

Shortly after he'd recovered I got really sick for about a week. Every day Josh sympathetically looked after my every need, never complaining and always happily helping and caring for me however he could.

It's fair to say that this was convicting! It made me realise that it's far better to *show* love (like Josh does) than to just *feel* it like I do. That's what the famous Scripture in 1 Corinthians 13 is all about:

Love is patient and kind. Love is not jealous or boastful or proud or rude. It does not demand its own way. It is not irritable, and it keeps no record of being wronged. It does not rejoice about injustice but rejoices whenever the truth wins out. Love never gives up, never loses faith, is always hopeful, and endures through every circumstance.
1 Corinthians 13:4-7

That's a love that is shown, not just felt.

Of course it's great to feel love too, but real love is one that outworks in actions, not just in sighs!

He is the right one

One of the books I read before getting married was by Dr Barry and Vanessa Chant called *Straight Talk about Marriage*. In it Dr Barry Chant tells a story about his wedding day. I'd like to quote it here:

"I often think back to my own wedding day. I can still picture myself standing before the mirror in my new grey suit, straightening my tie, and saying to myself, "I hope I'm doing the right thing!" Not that I was really thinking of backing out. I was 95 per cent sure that I was right. But I still raised the question.

"But then came the wedding service. We exchanged vows and gave ourselves to one another. There have been many, many good times since that day. There have also been some bad times.

But one thing I have never done again is to ask myself whether I did the right thing in marrying Vanessa. It's a question that no longer applies."[10]

I really like this. Why did the question of "Is she the right one for me?" no longer apply? Well, the way I see it Dr Barry had just declared his commitment to Vanessa in front of his family, friends and God. Therefore, she *was* the right one for him. There was no room for thinking: "Did I make the wrong choice?" By marrying her, she *was* the right choice.

This is a very powerful concept. So many women are so busy searching for their Mr Perfect. They think they've found him and marry him, or give up searching and settle for someone

10 *Straight Talk about Marriage*, Barry & Vanessa Chant, 1983, The House of Tabor, pp. 75-76

ACCEPT

else. Then years into their marriage they start to wonder if they married the wrong man.

By all means, before you get married do everything you can to make sure you choose a man who loves God and is committed to following Him, who shares similar interests to you, who you're attracted to and who is your best friend. That's just wise.

But once you are married, that's it. You have chosen this man; therefore, he *is* the right one. There is no other 'right one' floating around with whom you would have a much better life. Your husband *is* the right man for you. If you keep searching for 'the one', you will only go from man to man and be disappointed. There is no Mr Perfect, only your husband. Your challenge is to accept that he is the 'right one' for you.

So unless you have biblical grounds for divorce, I encourage you to stick it out and work at your marriage. No marriage is easy and it's even harder if perhaps you weren't as discerning as you could have been when you chose your husband. But you chose him and you committed yourself to him, so pray, pray, pray that God helps you to accept him as the 'right one' for you.

He won't read marriage books

As I've already said, I've written this book entirely for wives. There's no advice in here for husbands.

This is because so many women read marriage books and then try to force their husbands to read them. Or they try to make their husband watch a particularly relevant episode of a day-time relationship show. Or they drag their husband to a marriage enrichment weekend. The truth is, most men hate these things. It's like them forcing you to read their sports magazine, wanting you to watch the stock market channel with them or dragging you to a five day test match (sorry if these examples don't apply to your husband, but I'm sure you can think of some relevant examples). Most men aren't wired that way. Sitting around talking about their feelings is not interesting or exciting for them, just like sitting around discussing footy scores is not exciting for me! If you have a husband who does like reading marriage books, consider yourself very blessed.

Dr Emerson Eggerichs, the author of *Love & Respect*, talks about how a wife giving her husband a book on marriage is equivalent to a husband giving his wife a book on dieting. It's insulting! Men see their wife asking them to read a marriage book as criticism—they think it is their wife telling them they are a terrible husband[11].

---

11 *A Beginner's Guide to Understanding Your Spouse's Needs*, Emerson Eggerichs, 27 May 2015, retrieved from http://loveandrespect.com/blog/a-beginners-guide-to-understanding-your-spouses-needs/

So... if your husband decides to go to a marriage enrichment seminar, great. If not, get over it. If your husband flicks over to a great relationship show, great. If not, get over it. And don't even bother leaving marriage books lying around, open to a certain page with highlighted sections. Would you read it if it was a stock report or cricket magazine?

If you want to read marriage books, watch marriage videos or go to marriage seminars, by all means do it, but do it with a heart to learn how *you* can be a better wife, not to figure out all the things *he's* doing wrong as a husband. So many women read marriage books thinking: "Oh yes! If only he did this...yes, he should do that...if only I could get him to read this". Instead, we should be reading these books thinking: "*I* should do that..."

I'm hoping that after reading this book there's no chance of you thinking that the way to fix your marriage is by trying to fix your husband!

Thankfulness is better than frustration

Expectations about household tasks can be the cause of much conflict. Without realising it, both the husband and wife will often expect each other to do basically the same tasks as their mother or father did[12]. But your husband is not your father and, even if he is similar to your father, it is unlikely that he will have exactly the same skills and interests. Some men love to garden, others just do it to make their house look nice, and others hate it. Just like some women love to cook, some do it to stay alive, and others hate it!

When Josh and I first got married we started doing everything together. Over time, we naturally took ownership of the tasks we were interested in and then a few tasks that neither of us particularly wanted got picked up by whomever it irritated first! Because of this, most of the household tasks we do now are the ones that we are more interested in and care about. For example, Josh manages all the money and I do all the cleaning. I wouldn't say that either of us love these jobs, but Josh really cares about good money management, and I really care about a clean house. So it makes sense for us to do the jobs we care about the most.

One thing that we did conflict about initially was my belief that I was doing nearly all of the household tasks. As I was working full-time too I thought this was very unfair. It took me a really long time to realise all of the jobs that Josh actually did (When he tore the ligament in his ankle

---

12 See *He won't meet your expectations*.

ACCEPT

I quickly learnt how much he did, because I had to do it all!). Previously I hadn't counted things like filling up the car with petrol, getting the car serviced, paying the bills, managing our money, mowing the lawns and watering the garden as jobs. Yet these are all important. Just because I wasn't doing them didn't mean they weren't necessary for the functioning of our household! Once I started to realise all the things that Josh did I saw that our duties were almost exactly half and half—if anything, Josh was doing more than me.

Something I really regret about my first year of marriage is how I 'trained' Josh out of doing any indoor housework. Like I said, initially we did everything together and evenly. But I quickly trained him out of that by criticising everything he did. If he swept the floor I pointed out all the corners he'd missed. If he washed the dishes I would criticise the one dirty plate that slipped through. If he dried the dishes I would criticise the lack of dryness. If he put on a load of washing I would criticise him for not separating the whites from the darks. Yes, I trained him all right. I taught him that nothing he did was good enough. I taught him that he was better off not helping. So he stopped. That's about the time he started taking on more and more of the outside and non-cleaning type tasks, probably to get away from my criticising glare!

Now, of course, I've realised that I need to be grateful for any cleaning he does, especially now that I've taken it on as my responsibility. I need to let him do it his way and ignore the little things that are different from my way. Over the years Josh has begun to help me more and more with my cleaning duties as I've learnt to shut up more. It's still a challenge for me, but I'm learning to be grateful rather than critical.

An example of all of this is emptying the kitchen bin. As I was growing up this was always my dad's job, then later my brother's. So when I got married I just assumed this was Josh's job. I used to get very annoyed with Josh whenever the bin got really full. I don't think I ever told him this, I just got frustrated that he wasn't emptying it regularly! Then one day I had an 'ah-ha' moment and realised that there was no rulebook in the world that said it was his job. He didn't even know I thought it was his job! So I decided that I would make it my job, especially since I was the one who used it most frequently. I didn't say anything to Josh, I just mentally shifted 'Emptying the kitchen bin' from his list of jobs to mine.

This really helped change my attitude. Whenever the bin got full, I emptied it. Sometimes Josh would empty it before I got a chance to. When he did, I would be grateful because he'd done my job for me! In saying that, though, the other day I went to throw some rubbish in the bin but saw that there was no bin liner. My first instinct (Sad to say, after all these years!) was to get frustrated: "Argh! He's emptied the bin and not put another bin liner in!" Thankfully that was only for a split second, then I smiled, laughed at myself, and thanked God that I had a husband who saw that the bin was full and willingly emptied it for me (On a cold winter night too!) so that all I had to do was replace the liner. Appreciating him for what he does rather than focussing on what he doesn't do fills my heart with love and respect for him, rather than frustration and annoyance.

I realise that some husbands do very little (inside or outside). Sometimes they're actually just lazy or taking you for granted. Unfortunately, as we've already discussed, you can't change him and no amount of nagging will help. In this case I encourage you to pray. Ask God to help you appreciate what he *does* contribute to the house. Start thanking God (and your husband) for those things. Be grateful for what he does do instead of focussing on what he doesn't do.

On the flipside, are there jobs your husband is doing that he'd appreciate your help with? It doesn't hurt to ask. It might result in more work for you, but will also probably make him feel less annoyed towards you and more loving instead! Just as we love it when our husbands help us with our jobs, our husbands appreciate our help with their jobs.

No marriage is perfect

When you put two imperfect people in a house together for the rest of their lives, you *will* have conflict. This is normal and most people realise this.

However, some wives can have a misconception about marriage. They can think that to have a successful marriage they need to deal with every issue when it arises, they need to discuss all of their feelings, they need a totally transparent relationship and they need an intimacy of conversation at all levels.

While this would be nice, it is important to accept that your marriage will never be perfect. Until the day you die you will need to work on it. So why stress and worry about all of the imperfections in your relationship? Yes, work on them, but *at the right time*. You have a lifetime to work on them. Don't make every day a stress and a worry because you're forcing your husband to work through an issue with you.

Sometimes when Josh and I are in the middle of a disagreement something will happen to lighten the moment—maybe something interrupts us or one of us makes a joke, signalling that we don't really want to argue anymore. Sometimes it's okay to let it go. Laugh at the joke, turn the topic to something else. Not everything has to be sorted out today. Enjoy the good things you have. Probably leaving it for a few days or weeks might help give both of you a different perspective and allow you to address the issue with a better attitude and therefore a better result.

I'm not saying you should avoid the serious issues, but don't get all upset just because you and your husband don't have a perfect, soul-mate, best-friend-at-all-times relationship. No-one does!

ACCEPT

(not correct)

IN SUMMARY:

Don't try to change him

Get rid of all your expectations of him

Look to God, not your husband, to meet your needs

Only ask your husband something once (one reminder is okay!)

Focus on your own relationship with God, not his

Don't be his mother: remember it's his house too

Go to God for help, not your mum or friends

Ask God to help you empathise with your husband

Recognise that he is different, not wrong

Accept his quirks and temptations

Be content with real love and stop seeking the 'in love' feeling

Ask God to help you show love, not just feel it

Thank God that your husband is the 'right one' for you

Read marriage books for yourself, not to figure out what he's doing wrong

Don't get frustrated at what he doesn't do, be grateful for what he does do

Enjoy your marriage for what it is, focussing on the good

RESPECT

(not direct)

Ephesians 5:21-25, 28-33

And further, submit to one another out of reverence for Christ. For wives, this means submit to your husbands as to the Lord. For a husband is the head of his wife as Christ is the head of the church. He is the Savior of his body, the church. As the church submits to Christ, so you wives should submit to your husbands in everything.

For husbands, this means love your wives, just as Christ loved the church. He gave up his life for her...In the same way, husbands ought to love their wives as they love their own bodies. For a man who loves his wife actually shows love for himself. No one hates his own body but feeds and cares for it, just as Christ cares for the church. And we are members of his body. As the Scriptures say, "A man leaves his father and mother and is joined to his wife, and the two are united into one." This is a great mystery, but it is an illustration of the way Christ and the church are one. So again I say, each man must love his wife as he loves himself, and the wife must respect her husband.

1 Peter 3:1-6

In the same way, you wives must accept the authority of your husbands. Then, even if some refuse to obey the Good News, your godly lives will speak to them without any words. They will be won over by observing your pure and reverent lives. Don't be concerned about the outward beauty of fancy hairstyles, expensive jewellery, or beautiful clothes. You should clothe yourselves instead with the beauty that comes from within, the unfading beauty of a gentle and quiet spirit, which is so precious to God. This is how the holy women of old made themselves beautiful. They trusted God and accepted the authority of their husbands. For instance, Sarah obeyed her husband, Abraham, and called him her master. You are her daughters when you do what is right without fear of what your husbands might do.

Introduction

My eyes were opened to a husband's need for respect through the fantastic *Love & Respect* book written by Dr Emerson Eggerichs. This is a book every wife should read. It completely changed the way I understood Josh and my relationship with him.

In the Scriptures at the start of this section is a verse which is the basis of Dr Eggerich's book. Ephesians 5:33 says, "So again I say, each man must love his wife as he loves himself, and the wife must respect her husband".

Notice that it doesn't say "each man must love his wife, and the wife must love her husband"...which is a pity because that would be so much easier! But God does not command us to *love* our husbands. We are commanded to *respect* our husbands.

Why? Well, I'm going to generalise, but I believe the Bible says this because God knows what we need from our spouse! Even though men and women need both love and respect, men really desire and need respect, usually even more than love, and women really desire and need love, usually even more than respect. For example, consider the armed forces and raising children. The armed forces, which traditionally has been predominately made up of men, is all about respect and honour. Raising children, which has traditionally been predominately done by women, is all about love and nurture.

Men need respect and more naturally give respect, while women need love and more naturally give love. Think about it. It's true! Respect for men is like love for women.

Unfortunately this usually means that often women find it hard to show respect to their husbands and often husbands find it hard to show love to their wives.

I think wives find it especially hard to respect as our culture constantly bombards us with the message that respect has to be *earned*. This is ingrained in us. It would not seem unreasonable to most people for a wife to say to her husband: "You need to earn my respect. I'm not going to give it to you unless you deserve it."

But the Bible doesn't say, "The wife must respect her husband *if he deserves it*", just as it doesn't say, "Each man must love his wife as he loves himself *if she deserves it*". We're called to do it irrespective of merit.

Imagine if you were told by your husband, "You need to earn my love; I'm not going to give it to you unless you deserve it". What a horrible way to live your married life! You want to know that he loves you even when you stuff up. *Especially* when you stuff up. The same goes for our husbands. They need to know we respect them, even when they make mistakes. *Especially* when they make mistakes!

Our husbands need us to respect them. God knew what He was talking about! He told us to respect our husbands, because He knew that respect would enable them to be the strong, wise, kind men that He wants (and we want) them to be.

As I said, understanding what this means has changed the way I think about marriage. You see what I want from my husband more than anything is love. I want to hear him tell me he loves me, I want him to show that he loves me with the things he does, I want to be absolutely, one hundred percent sure, that he loves me at all times. I just assumed that Josh wanted the same thing from me, which is why I couldn't understand why he didn't like me telling him all the time that I loved him. Now I realise that I was smothering him with my love when really what he wanted and needed was my respect!

Instead of showing respect, most wives (myself included) find themselves telling their husbands what to do, bossing them around and forcing them to do what they want. Clearly, this is not healthy.

So how can we **respect** our husbands rather than **direct** them? This section will give some suggestions for how you can show him the respect he needs.

But...before you turn the page please be aware that this is probably going to be the hardest section in this book to read, believe and apply. Before turning the page please take a deep breath and ask God to help you as you read.

Don't say I didn't warn you! ☺

Submission is great

A couple of months before I got married my mum had a big talk with me. She sat me down and said she was seriously concerned about where my marriage was headed. She had been observing how Josh and I interacted and how I constantly pushed to get my own way. Josh and I are both very strong willed, but because he loved me, he would often give me what I wanted. She was worried about the long term effect this would have on our marriage and so she began to tell me what I should be doing instead.

I was not very impressed with what mum had to say. I thought it was very unfair of her to try to tell me what to do. I was nineteen and an engaged woman!

Thankfully, though, God opened my ears to hear what she was saying, even though I didn't like it. By the end of our conversation, I realised that what my mum was telling me was the truth. I thank God so much for what she taught me that day. Without it, I dread to think what kind of marriage I'd have today—if any!

What did she tell me? Well, she taught me something that is foundational to any good marriage. She taught me something that our current culture frowns upon but the Bible teaches us to do.

She taught me about the necessity and value of submission.

Now I know submission is a very unpopular topic[13]. That's because the word submission usually brings to mind

---

13 If it helps, whenever you read the word 'submission', replace it with the word 'respect', because essentially true submission is giving your husband true respect!

images of weakness, of a woman kneeling in the dirt, of a bowed head, of a slave. This, however, is not what Biblical submission is all about. So, even though I know a lot of women get agitated when I talk to them about submission, I am going to write about it. I'm writing about it because it was the first thing I learnt that really changed my marriage for the better and because a lack of submission is one of the biggest problems in most marriages today.

I hope you can read this fairly long topic with an open heart and mind. I'm first of all going to explain why Biblical submission is necessary, then I'll explain what it is and then I'll give some examples of how this has worked out in my life.

As a corporate trainer I teach staff about approaches to conflict using the following model[14]:

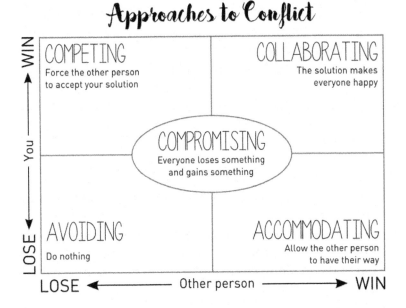

Approaches to Conflict

COMPETING
Force the other person
to accept your solution

COLLABORATING
The solution makes
everyone happy

COMPROMISING
Everyone loses something
and gains something

AVOIDING
Do nothing

ACCOMMODATING
Allow the other person
to have their way

WIN — You — LOSE

LOSE ← Other person → WIN

14 Adapted from *Key Steps in Collaborative Problem Solving*, Judy Worrell, http://www.affinitymc.com/collaborative_problem_solving.htm, retrieved on 29 July 2004

The example I would always use was of a couple who had conflict over the toothpaste. The wife was very neat and pedantic. She liked the toothpaste to be squeezed evenly from the bottom of the tube and the top to be wiped after each use to prevent the build-up of dried toothpaste. The husband would just grab the tube and squeeze wherever, squirting toothpaste everywhere. The wife can either avoid the situation (just hope he will miraculously change one day), accommodate (say "OK, fine, squeeze it however you like"), compete (demand that he does it the *right* way) or compromise (suggest that he tries to be more careful and she'll try to relax her expectations). The point of the illustration is that none of those methods are ideal. Instead, they should go for the win-win which is collaborating, that is working together to find a solution that will make them both happy. The answer is easy: get two tubes of toothpaste. Yay! Problem solved!

This sounds all lovely but unfortunately it often takes a long time to come up with a collaborative solution and, furthermore, a collaborative solution is not always possible to find. As I used to explain to the staff, you may end up settling for a compromise, or, if the person you are conflicting with is your manager, they may end up competing, that is, forcing you to do as they want since they are the boss!

What about in a marriage? What if you can't agree on a decision that you need to make? What if you can't find a collaborative, win-win solution? 'Compromise' is the word that is often touted but I believe this is a second-rate answer. In this approach, nobody wins. And usually one person ends up 'compromising' more than the other which can build resentment.

Let's look at a bigger issue than toothpaste. Let's say a couple decide they want to buy a new car. Their old car is getting expensive to fix and they have $20,000 saved in the bank. There's just one little problem. She really wants a brand new nice, sleek sedan with all the bells and whistles while he wants a second-hand 4WD that will be a good solid car. The wife will usually take one of these five approaches:

1. Avoid

She might hate conflict and therefore might suggest they hold off buying a new car until they can decide what to do. Why buy a new car when they can run the existing one into the ground? This approach is not solving the conflict, just leaving it until another day. Therefore, it's a 'Lose—Lose' result.

2. Compete

She can keep going on and on about how stupid it is to get another second hand car that will also break down. She can argue that they live in the city and that a 4WD is useless in the city. She can cry about how hard and scary it will be for her to drive and park such a big, high car. She can tell him that a brand new car, with a 3 year warranty is a much better investment as they won't have to pay for break downs. She can point out the great features like cruise control, climate control and airbags for safety. She can explain that when they have kids a sedan is much easier to put kids in and out of. In other words, she can overwhelm him to the point that he feels forced to buy the kind of car she wants. She may even just go out and buy the car she wants, leaving him no say whatsoever. This (apparently) is a 'Win—Lose' result. She wins, he loses.

Except, of course, that is not the case. She might get the car she wants, but then when they are offered the loan of a caravan for a free holiday he'll say, "Sorry, can't do it. We don't have a 4WD". When they go camping with their friends and some of the guys go four-wheel driving, he will look resentfully at his wife when he has to miss out. It will always be a source of disappointment and frustration to him that he didn't get the car he wanted. And any time something goes wrong with the brand new sedan (for example, if it struggles to get up big hills) he will say, "I told you this car would be rubbish!" Neither of them will end up enjoying the new car.

3. Accommodate

She can unwillingly say, "Fine. Get whatever car you want". (Which of course is code for "...but that better be the car I want!"). He will happily take that as a go ahead to get the 4WD he wants. Then every time the 4WD is hard to park or breaks down she will complain. In fact, whenever anything about it isn't perfect, she'll let him know all about it. Again, it's meant to be a 'Lose—Win' result where he wins and she loses, but in reality they both lose.

4. Compromise

They can get a loan so they can afford to get a brand new 4WD with some of the bells and whistles to keep her happy and the 4WD part to keep him happy. But they will have to spend more than they want to. And she still won't like that it's big. And he won't like that she won't allow him to take it off road for fear of scratching it. Again, nobody wins.

5. Collaborate

Buy two cars! Yay! Lovely in theory, but it is not going to happen in practice. Sure people with lots of money may be able to go down this path, but not most couples. Certainly not couples with only $20,000 saved.

Clearly, none of these approaches are ideal. There has to be a better way. There is! It's Biblical submission.

The Bible is very clear about submission. It says in Colossians:

> Wives, submit to your husbands, as is fitting for those who belong to the Lord.
> **Colossians 3:18**

God loves women as much as he loves men. When He gave this command, He did so for a good purpose, which was to help women have a great marriage (as you'll see), not to make their lives a misery.

The picture of a woman being a weak slave, domineered over by her husband is not submission, but subjugation. That is not what I'm talking about.

This is how I define Biblical submission:

Choosing to respect your husband by empowering him to make the final decision.

I want to clarify what Biblical submission is and isn't:

- **Submission cannot be demanded, it is a choice**

  A husband cannot demand that his wife submit to him, just like a wife cannot demand that her husband love her. A wife has to choose each time there is difference of opinion whether she will submit or not.

- **Submission is not a sign of weakness, it takes great strength**

  It takes great, great, great strength to empower your husband to make the final decision. Especially when you really care about the outcome of the decision.

- **Submission is not being quiet, it's sharing your thoughts and opinions**

  You should not stay quiet, just letting your husband decide whatever he wants. Your opinions and needs are valuable and important! Your husband needs to hear what you have to say. You should definitely share what you think in a calm and nice way. (Don't go on and on about it though!)

  To balance this you should actively look for the positives in his viewpoint as well. This is key. When you start to focus on the good in his preference (rather than the bad), God can really help you change your attitude. You may even end up agreeing with him and then submission is no longer necessary! Even if you still think your option is the best, it will make submission so much easier if you can look for the positives in his option. If you can't find any positives, ask God. He will show you! I'll give you an example shortly.

- **Submission is not giving in, it's giving your husband respect**

  It is a very empowering experience for your husband when you tell him your opinions but then genuinely say: "It's up to you honey. I trust you to make the best decision for us". Not only are you giving him the freedom to make the decision, but you are telling him that you, his wife, trust him to make the right decision. This is giving him respect.

A woman I know had a husband who would agree to pretty much everything she wanted. But she got so frustrated with him because she felt she had to make all the decisions in their marriage. She was annoyed that her husband wasn't decisive and that he didn't take control. Once she understood the concept of submission, however, her whole attitude changed. She suddenly realised that a big part of the reason he had become this weak kind of man she despised was because she'd never let him decide anything. And she'd never let him decide because she hadn't trusted him to make the right decision. It was very difficult for her to change, but she realised that instead of deciding for him, she needed to give him respect by letting him take control. When she did this, she really was still 'in control'. She still made the choice to let him decide each time they didn't agree. Doing this was difficult, but it was also incredibly empowering for both her and her husband.

- **Submission is not trusting your husband's wisdom, but trusting God's wisdom**

Our husbands don't know everything and sometimes we will know more than them about a decision because we have researched it more or because we have more experience. That's why it's so hard to hand the control over to someone else. But the beautiful thing about submission is that the 'someone else' you are handing control over to is not your husband, but God. This is what the following Scripture is all about:

> This is how the holy women of old made themselves beautiful. They trusted God and accepted the authority of their husbands. For instance, Sarah obeyed her husband, Abraham, and called him her

master. You are her daughters when you do what is right without fear of what your husbands might do.
1 Peter 3:5-6

When we submit to our husbands we are putting the outcome in God's hands and trusting Him to make it work out for the best. We can (and should!) pray that God will give our husband wisdom to make the right decision and then we just need to trust that God will do so. Our husbands will no doubt make mistakes when they make decisions. But we do not need to be afraid. God is good and can *always* be trusted to do what is right and best for you both in the long run. I strongly believe He will honour our submission. He has never failed me yet.

Every time that I have submitted to Josh, God has made it work out right. Even when I am totally convinced that my opinion is correct but have submitted and Josh has decided to not follow my suggestion, it has *always* worked out for the best. Things have occurred that would have made my decision a bad one, or things have happened that have made Josh's decision clearly right. This only serves to reinforce my trust in God, my respect for Josh and Josh's confidence in his decision-making ability. These are all excellent things!

Every time that I have not submitted to Josh, things seem to go from bad to worse. The decision that I *knew* was right suddenly doesn't work out. Then *I'm* responsible for the negative outcomes and I wind up feeling terribly guilty (especially if it was a decision that cost lots of money or time). Unfortunately, I often don't even realise I'm not submitting until it's too late. And each time I don't submit it deflates Josh and causes strain in our relationship.

When I was pregnant with our first child Josh was asked to be a groomsman at a wedding in Bali. I really wanted to go but our baby would only be about four months old at the time of the wedding. I thought that would be okay, we would cope. Josh thought it was a bad idea. In the end I said, "It's up to you hon". He then went and bought tickets...for himself. I was really disappointed. However, I ended up being so, so glad he didn't listen to me! Our beautiful baby daughter cut her first tooth the day before the wedding and her second tooth the day before Josh travelled home. She did not cope well. There was a lot of screaming, whinging and pain for days before and after each tooth. Neither Josh nor I could have predicted that she would get her teeth that early, but God knew! He gave Josh the wisdom to make the right decision.

- **Submission is not complaining about his decision, but being positive about his decision**

  If we submit but then whinge and complain about his decision we're actually not submitting! Submission is not so much about your actions as it is about your attitude[15]. It is not sulkily saying: "Fine, whatever, you decide", it is a conscious decision to be happy with whatever your husband decides. It is finding the positives in his suggestion and then actively and happily helping him to implement the decision he makes.

  I remember when we bought our house in Darwin. The front yard was a mess so we decided to bulldoze it and start from scratch. It had an old front fence which I thought was great because it provided an enclosed front yard for kids to play in, which would be a good

---

15 John Bevere's book and DVD, *Undercover*, goes into great detail about how obedience (an action) and submission (an attitude) work together. I highly recommend reading the book or watching the DVD series if you can.

feature when we sold one day. I had drawn plan after plan of how we could design our new front yard and fix up the fence to make it a real feature. Then Josh told me that he wanted to get rid of the front fence. I explained to him why I thought we should keep it, but then said to him: "I trust you though; we'll do whatever you think is best. If you think we should get rid of it, let's do that". (Mind you, this was after a lot of prayer and wrestling with God about this whole situation!) Josh then drove me around some of the nicer suburbs in Darwin and I saw that nearly all of the expensive and nice homes had no front fence. I actively looked for the positives and then told him what they were: it opened up the front of the house, making it look more attractive; it would save us having to pay to fix it up; and it would mean not having to open a gate every time we drove in or out of the driveway. By the end of the trip, I was entirely convinced that the fence should go! We didn't have to rip it down for another month or so, but from then on all of my front yard designs did not include a fence.

However, a few weeks later Josh told me that because of all the dogs in the neighbourhood and the amount of young kids around, he'd decided a front fence was a good idea after all. So it stayed.

I don't tell that story as an example of how submission can help you get your own way. I tell it because it made me laugh. You see, by the time Josh had decided to go with what I wanted, I was convinced that his way was right instead! In my heart, I had truly submitted and was entirely happy with whatever decision he made. This is a great place to be and I love it when I get there (I don't always). Then you have real peace and real joy, whatever the outcome of your husband's decision, because you can see the positives in both ways.

- **Submission is not based on your husband's spirituality, but on your obedience**

  You might be wondering what you should do if your husband isn't a Christian or if he is a Christian but doesn't seem to be very spiritual. The following Scripture is very helpful:

  > In the same way, you wives must accept the authority of your husbands. Then, even if some refuse to obey the Good News, your godly lives will speak to them without any words. They will be won over by observing your pure and reverent lives.
  > **1 Peter 3:1-2**

  I strongly believe that God will honour the decisions your husband makes when you submit because you are being obedient to God. I do encourage you to pray, though, that God will give your husband wisdom[16].

Now that I've explained what I mean by submission, let's look again at the example of a couple who want two different types of cars. The wife now has a new option: to *submit*. She can choose to explain nicely to her husband why she would like the sedan and ask him to explain why the 4WD is so important to him. She can then ask God to help her find the positives in a 4WD and ask God to give her husband wisdom to choose the best car for their family, whatever that is. Then she can say to her husband: "Honey, I'm really happy for you to decide what to get. I think there are positives both ways." Then when they go looking at

---

16 However, we should not submit to our husbands if they ask us to do something that is clearly contrary to God's Word, for example, if they ask us to lie, cheat or steal. We should respectfully decline.

cars she should actively go look at the 4WDs and only look at the sedans if her husband leads the way!

Now, if her husband decides to get the 4WD, she will be happy—because she has trusted that God will make this the best decision. She already knows what the positives are for having a 4WD and can thank God that she now has a car that is safe and a car that they can take out camping. (Great! An opportunity for some fun quality time!)

And if her husband ends up deciding to get the sedan, he won't be whinging and complaining if anything goes wrong because *he* decided to get it. He may have decided that her reasons for a sedan made good sense, or he may have chosen to get the sedan because he loves his wife and wants her to be happy. Whatever the reason, he has bought the sedan because he wanted to, not because he was forced into it. He has done so willingly and happily.

It really doesn't matter now whether they get the sedan or the 4WD. Either way, there's no conflict, there's no "I told you so". Both of them WIN.

Submission is incredibly powerful!

You know, before my little chat with mum I hadn't really given any thought as to who 'ran' my relationship with Josh. We just made decisions as they arose and whoever cared the most kept pushing until they won. Usually that was me. It slowly became clear to me that unless my attitude changed I would either have a dominated husband or we would constantly be fighting. Given Josh's personality, it would definitely be the latter. This was not the kind of marriage I wanted, so I decided from that day that I would learn to submit.

When I told Josh about my conversation with mum and explained to him that I wanted to submit to him when we were married, I was amazed at how relieved he was. He admitted that it had been the one major concern he'd had about marrying me. I hadn't even realised it was an issue.

I would love to say that from the day I was married I always submitted to my husband, but that is far from the truth. With my very strong will (and a very strong sense of *always* being right!) submission is a daily struggle. But every time I submit I am so happy and glad that I did. And every time I don't submit I regret it. Thankfully, God is helping me, and slowly (oh, so slowly) I'm getting better at it. I hope that you, too, can take this word of advice, as I did from my mum, and see the value in submission. This changed attitude will definitely change your marriage for the better.

He needs to be free to make mistakes

Everybody makes mistakes. Nobody is perfect. And *everybody* hates being told "I told you so". Nothing will stifle your husband more than continually reminding him of his mistakes. It will wear down his confidence and undermine his authority. Remember—men need **respect**. Without it he will become less and less able to make decisions.

So, if you've submitted to him (or even if you haven't) and he's made a decision that hasn't worked out the way he expected, you should say...nothing. He's smart enough to realise he made a mistake and he probably feels embarrassed. And I don't mean give him the silent treatment—it's something you should just get over. You make mistakes too! Think about how you would want him to respond when you make mistakes and do the same for him. Forgive him then forget about it. If he asks you what you think, have an, "Oh well, it doesn't matter" attitude, or if that's not appropriate to the situation, say whatever tells him "It's okay, I still respect you" ("I still love you" is not what he needs at this time).

This is very difficult when you have done the right thing by submitting and he's made a poor decision. Especially if that poor decision costs you significant amounts of time and money. But I want to encourage you to look for any positive outcomes from the poor decision. God has an amazing way of working all things together for good for those who love Him and are called according to His purpose (Romans 8:28)! Usually you will be able to look back later and thank God that you submitted because of the good that came from it.

If you respond positively and respectfully when your husband makes mistakes, it will encourage him more than you can imagine. He will feel like you 'have his back', giving him the confidence he needs to make good decisions in the future.

Forcing him won't work

It's a bad idea to try to force your husband to do something. For example:

- Attend a marriage enrichment conference with you
- Go out to dinner at someone's house
- Attend a play/performance with you
- Have a devotional time with you every day
- Go to bed when you do

Now, these may all seem like reasonable things to expect a husband to do. They may also seem like really good things to do. For example, going out to dinner will really help that new couple in the church feel connected. And having a regular devotional time together is so important for building a healthy marriage, isn't it? Not to mention going to a marriage enrichment conference!

Even though these are good things in themselves, we have to remember that no one likes being forced. It's human nature. Something in us resists being forced, even if it's something we might otherwise have been happy to do.

Let's say you are successful in dragging your husband along to a marriage enrichment conference. Is he going to enjoy himself? Is he going to get anything out of it? Chances are he'll be so annoyed that he'll go out of his way to find anything and everything about the conference that has been poorly delivered or organised. Then he will make a point of mentioning each and every one of those things to you whenever he possibly can throughout the conference. The end result will probably be a self-righteous husband who says, "I *told* you this would be a waste of time" and you'll be frustrated because he missed all the 'bits' that you thought he needed to hear.

None of this will enrich your marriage!

The same goes for all the other examples. If you push your husband hard enough, chances are you will be able to force him to do what you want. But do you really want him doing something just because you made him? Or do you want him to do it because he *wants* to?

You know, it's a bit like the way God was with us. He could have forced us all to do what is right all the time. Instead He gave us free will so that we could choose whether or not we wanted to do what was pleasing to Him. The risk of us sometimes choosing to do wrong was worth it for the times that we would choose, out of our own free will, to do what was right.

So, feel free to ask your husband if he wants to do something that you would like him to do, but don't make it sound like an order. Don't *direct* him, instead *respect* his feelings! Be genuinely willing to not go to the conference, dinner or play if he doesn't want to go. Don't sulk about it if he says no. Go to the play with a girlfriend and enjoy some 'girl time'. Do your devotion times by yourself. Make the most of your 'alone' bed time by reading your Bible or a good book. See the positives.

You never know. If your husband doesn't feel forced, he might just surprise you one day by saying yes. Then, when he does what you were wanting he will do it happily, out of his own will, and there is a good chance he will enjoy it. And if he doesn't enjoy it, he won't blame you!

On the flipside, is there anything that your husband has been trying to force you to do? Do you do it with complaints and grumbling? Do you whinge about it at every opportunity to your mum, girlfriends and/or random strangers? Do you drag your heels and make it really, really clear that you really, really don't want to do it?

Do what you'd love him to do: smile, be happy, think of the positives and tell him all the good things about it. Pray beforehand that God will help you do all of these things genuinely. You'll be amazed how much you may enjoy whatever it was you were reluctant to do. And if it doesn't work out, your husband is unlikely to get upset because he'll see that you at least you tried.

Correcting him is disrespectful

I'm always right. Unfortunately, Josh is always right too, which means that, at least some of the time, one of us might think we're right when we're actually wrong. And, shock, horror, it's often me.

The safest way for me to not look stupid is to watch what I say. More importantly, I need to be very, very careful about correcting my husband. In fact, I'm slowly learning that I should NEVER do it in public. Let me tell you a true story:

JOSH: (To one of his friends) Yeah, the house prices are booming in Darwin. The housing commission house around the corner from us just sold for $315,000.

SALLY: (Knowing he's exaggerating, and wanting the story to be accurate) $290,000...

JOSH: No, it was $315,000.

SALLY: (Gently, with a 'please be patient' smile at the friend) I'm sure it only went for $290,000. I was at the auction with you.

JOSH: (With annoyance) I wasn't talking about that house, I was talking about the other one, opposite the power station.

SALLY: (Feeling small and stupid) Oh...

End result? I make myself look stupid, I make Josh look stupid and it is only going to (rightly so) make Josh annoyed with me.

We should honour our husbands, not correct them in front of others. It is much better to shut our mouths! I should have remembered this verse:

> Watch your tongue and keep your mouth shut, and you will stay out of trouble.
> **Proverbs 21:23**

If you're really concerned that a detail is wrong you can ask him about it later when no-one is around. It certainly saves embarrassment if you're wrong!

It's not nice to be bossy

I'm bossy. Unfortunately, I usually have no idea that I'm being bossy. I think the first time I was really made aware of it was when I was 17 at a Pastor's Kid's camp. I was talking with some of the other campers about the different personality types: choleric (leader, visionary, controlling), sanguine (lively, friendly, talkative), melancholy (artistic, thoughtful, moody) and phlegmatic (laid back, calm, indecisive). I said that I was sanguine/choleric and one of the other campers said, "No, you're choleric/sanguine. You're more 'bossy' than 'life of the party'."

I was shattered.

I didn't like it, but she was right. I *can* be incredibly bossy. And this is not just with my family, work colleagues and friends, it's also (and especially!) with my husband. Years ago God showed me how bossy I was being towards him. Below is an extract from my journal at that time, which was written while we were renovating our house:

22/3/05

Now that I'm conscious that I boss Josh, I see it ALL the time. I boss him every minute of the day. And the worst thing is, last night I was praying to you and thinking: "God help me not to boss Josh"...then we started to do the dishes and tidy up and Josh started wiping down our concrete-dust covered benches with the new dishcloth I'd gotten out, instead of the old one I'd 'allocated' for this job. So I was like: "Uh, uh—Stop! Don't use that one! That's gross! Use this one instead!" Then, "Don't put the tea-towel on the dirty bench" and so on and so forth. As I was speaking I realised I was being bossy, but I figured that I was in the right and that it was worth it, so I went right on. Of course, about five minutes later I realised that it wasn't worth it and that I have no right to boss Josh. It's his house. He can use whatever dishcloth he wants! At most I could have got the old dishcloth and put it down near him and said (nicely!) "Did you want to use this one instead?" Even that's a little bossy, but not as bad. God help me! I apologised to him but he's probably given up hoping I'll change. Help me God to change!!

It's so ridiculous when I look at it now. All that stress over a 15 cent dishcloth. It's not like he was using my wedding dress or something valuable! Instead I should have been grateful that he was cleaning up the mess.

I guess my point is that being bossy is never nice and husbands certainly don't like it. We shouldn't be telling our husbands what time they have to be home or who they can hang out with or how to drive a car. We need to respect their ability to decide these things for themselves. And if the decisions they make are different from our own opinions, we need to learn to let it go. Especially when it's over silly things like dishcloths!

(Hmm, interesting how we seem to argue over dishcloths! ☺)

He thrives on giving advice

Something I've always found challenging is knowing how to respond when I've asked my husband for advice but then I don't agree with the advice he gives me. I'm sure most of us find this hard! This is where we have to remember our husband's need for respect. If we dismiss or disregard his advice it shows we don't respect his views, opinions or ideas.

So...what to do? One solution is to never ask your husband for advice, then there is no quandary. But I think this means we miss out on a very valuable opportunity to not only get fantastic advice but also build up our husband.

Let me explain. Let's say there's a situation and you don't know what to do. The first thing you should always do is pray about it. But if you're like me, it's sometimes hard to separate your feelings from God's voice. Here's where your husband can help. Ask God to give *your husband* wisdom and the right advice for you. Then ask God to help you accept and follow whatever advice your husband gives. This is really important, because chances are he'll say something different from what you think.

Now, you may think this is scary. It is! It's putting your trust in someone else. But, don't be mistaken, it's *God* you're putting your trust in, *not* your husband. God is perfect, all knowing and can always be trusted to do what is right and best.

The following passage, which I referred to earlier, applies here too:

RESPECT

This is how the holy women of old made themselves beautiful. They trusted God and accepted the authority of their husbands. For instance, Sarah obeyed her husband, Abraham, and called him her master. You are her daughters when you do what is right without fear of what your husbands might do.

1 Peter 3:5-6

God calls us to *do what is right* (that is, obey our husbands) *without fear of what our husbands might do.* Why can we do this? That is, why can we obey without being afraid that our husband will give us the wrong advice? Because we put our trust in **God**[17]*.

If you've prayed and asked God to give your husband wisdom, then when you ask your husband for advice you can do so knowing that whatever he says is God's advice to you. Then you just need to follow his advice! The end result will be that you have done the right thing (because you've had the right advice) and you will have shown your husband that you respect him and his advice, consequently building your marriage. Great for you and great for him!

17 *Even if your husband is not a Christian I believe you can still trust God to give him the wisdom to give the right advice. Make sure you do pray first, though, that God gives him wisdom.

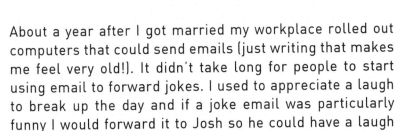

Mocking men isn't helpful

About a year after I got married my workplace rolled out computers that could send emails (just writing that makes me feel very old!). It didn't take long for people to start using email to forward jokes. I used to appreciate a laugh to break up the day and if a joke email was particularly funny I would forward it to Josh so he could have a laugh too.

One time, though, I forwarded him an email which I thought was hilarious and I was surprised when he emailed me back saying something along the lines of, "I can't believe you'd think this is funny". Taken aback, I read the joke again. I can't remember the joke now but the punchline was, like many of the jokes I'd been receiving, that men are stupid, ha, ha. Josh's response made me realise for the first time that men don't find these sorts of jokes funny.

Of course I should have realised that. I don't think jokes about women being stupid are funny. I don't think any woman does (unless she tells it about herself). In fact, for years women have fought to be taken seriously by men. They have fought to be able to vote, to work and to have equal pay. They fought against discrimination, sexual harassment and stereotyping. They fought to have playboy calendars removed from workplaces and to stop men from treating women like ditsy airheads, only good for cooking, cleaning and sex.

But now that men can get sacked for joking about women or objectifying them, some women have gone one step further and decided to treat men exactly the same way they hated being treated! And of course, it's not just emails. Men are put down as being dumb and stupid in social media, TV shows, movies, magazines...the list goes on.

There's a simple test as to whether a joke or statement about men is funny or offensive. Change the word from 'man' to 'woman' and now see if you think it is funny or not.

Our words and actions should encourage men to be who God has called them to be. We should be aiming to respect them, honour them and celebrate their differences. Laughing at men and mocking them will only discourage them from trying. It deflates them and disrespects them. I'm not saying you can't have fun and joke around—of course you can and should! But I encourage you to not share jokes that disrespect men.

He needs you to be his biggest fan

Imagine you found out that your husband had told his mates that you were "letting yourself go", that you were a terrible cook and that you were always nagging him. No doubt you'd be furious. Not just because he thought these things but because he'd been so cruel as to tell them to someone else.

We wouldn't like it done to us, yet so many women complain about their husbands to their friends, work colleagues and parents. Why do we do it? Maybe we're upset at something they've done or we just want an understanding ear. However, I think that saying *anything* unkind about your husband to *anyone* is a huge no-no[18]. It's all about respect!

In addition to not saying bad things to other people, you need to make sure you're saying positive things to other people. You need to be your husband's biggest fan! This means believing the good things about your husband and only repeating those things. However, you do need to be careful about going over the top. Some men are quite uncomfortable with public praise and it can also appear boastful if you keep talking about how good your husband is. A simple rule of thumb is that if your husband heard you talking about him it should result in him feeling either nothing or pleasure—not pain!

This goes for when you're speaking to your husband as well. Don't laugh at his mistakes, mock him or make

---

18 If you really feel the need to talk to someone about the problems you have with your husband, see *God is your best counsellor*.

him feel small. This will only reinforce his weaknesses. Instead, build him up by encouraging him, respecting him and praising him...of course you need to make sure you do this genuinely and not in a patronising manner.

Also, remember that submission is an attitude. When submitting it's not enough to go along with what your husband says but then tell everyone: "Sorry, I know this is dumb, but this is what my husband wants me to do". This is putting him down, not respecting him. True submission means looking for the positives in the decision and promoting those, not complaining about all the negatives.

Finally, if someone criticises your husband in front of you, defend him, just as you would like him to defend you. Don't lie or excuse his mistakes, but you can always try to help the other person understand your husband's perspective. This is especially important if it is one of your family members who is criticising your husband. They need to understand that you are on your husband's side first.

After all, if you're not his biggest fan, who is?

RESPECT

(not direct)

IN SUMMARY:

Give him respect with your words and actions

Choose to let him make the final decision when you don't agree

Be gracious when he makes mistakes, don't rub it in

Don't force him to do anything

Don't correct him in front of other people

Respect his ability to make decisions for himself, don't boss him around

Pray, ask your husband for advice, then do what he advises

Say only respectful things about men in general

Say only positive things about your husband to others—be his biggest fan

CONNECT

(not neglect)

Philippians 2:4
Don't look out only for your own interests, but take an interest in others, too.

Ephesians 4:31-32
Get rid of all bitterness, rage, anger, harsh words, and slander, as well as all types of evil behaviour. Instead, be kind to each other, tenderhearted, forgiving one another, just as God through Christ has forgiven you.

Introduction

A few years ago, when my daughter was about 4 years old, God showed me how important this idea of connection is. Back then, by the time I got my daughter in bed, the dishes done and the washing hung out, it would be about 9.00pm. After that I figured it was *my* time. I would read, go on the computer or watch TV with Josh. But often Josh was watching shows I didn't really like so I started watching my own shows on our other little TV. I was quite happy with this arrangement as it gave me some time to myself and also let me catch up on some 'girl' shows that I loved.

After a while I began to realise we were living increasingly separate lives. In fact that phrase kept bouncing around my head, "Increasingly separate lives, increasingly separate lives, increasingly separate lives". It's fair to say that this scared me. We still loved each other, but were not really spending much time alone together.

Around this time I read *His Needs, Her Needs* by Willard F. Harley. This book really challenged me and one of the things it spoke about was the need for men to have recreational companionship with their wives. I hadn't realised that men really need and want to connect with their wives through leisure activities.

Before Josh and I had children we had lots of leisure activities in common: going to the movies, camping, travelling, visiting art galleries, eating out, hanging out with our friends and so on. But once we had kids, all of these things were a lot harder, especially when they were young. We went to the movies maybe once a year. We went on a holiday to Hobart when our daughter was two years old and it was a disaster. We just spent the whole time going to playgrounds and the one time we tried to go to an art gallery we had to leave because she kept touching the really expensive paintings. And going out for dinner, which is usually one of my favourite parts of a holiday, was incredibly stressful. Each night we'd spend the whole time trying to keep her occupied then scoff down our food so we could get her back to the hotel. What a waste of money with a young child!

Reading this book made me realise that Josh and I had very few interests in common that we could enjoy together while our daughter was young. This was pretty worrying.

Harley was pretty clear. He wasn't saying that a wife should just pretend to like doing the same things as her husband. Instead he suggested that they should try to find new things they both like doing together.

I began praying about it. I asked God to show me what leisure activities I should try that Josh would like.

Shortly after this, Josh told me that Foxtel was showing all of the new Dr Who seasons from 2005 onwards. He said he was going to record them and give them a try. I was scornful, "Dr Who?! That's a show for nerds! Who wants to watch that?!"

Anyway, I saw some of the first two episodes and didn't hate the show like I thought I would, but I also didn't love it. Then one night Josh told me he was going to watch the third episode if I wanted to see it. I was in the study, about to get some work done that I really wanted to do. I remember sitting there, torn. I really did not care about watching Dr Who and I *did* care about what I was working on. But tugging on my heart was the need to spend some 'fun' time with my husband. So after a couple of minutes of too-ing and fro-ing, I somewhat begrudgingly went out and watched the third episode with him.

But after a couple more episodes, I was hooked. I loved it! (And, before you mock me—if you're a naysayer like I was—you can't judge it until you watch it! It's a great show!) Anyway, we then proceeded to watch seven seasons of Dr Who together over the next few months.

If I had stayed at my computer that night and given up on Dr Who, I shudder to think how many more nights over the next year we would have spent apart. Instead, most nights once all my work was done, I'd join Josh in the lounge room and we'd watch one, two or even three episodes. Together. We'd look at each other and laugh at the funny parts. We'd talk about the plot lines together. I began to feel so much closer to him. Our common interest was drawing us together.

Once I got the hang of this idea of making an effort to connect with (rather than neglect) my husband, I began to find some other interests that we had in common. Because of this we now spend nearly every night together. Now instead of seeing the evenings as **my** time, I see them as **our** time.

Guess what? I LOVE it!

And so does he ☺.

Connecting with your husband is more than just watching TV shows together or having common interests (although this is a big part of it). As it says in Ephesians 4:

> Verse 31: Get rid of all bitterness, rage, anger, harsh words, and slander, as well as all types of evil behaviour.

Verse 32: Instead, be kind to each other, tenderhearted, forgiving one another, just as God through Christ has forgiven you.

Ephesians 4:31-32

We can ask ourselves if our marriage more closely resembles the words in verse 31 or the words in verse 32. We can have a hundred interests in common with our husband, but if we are bitter, angry and harsh towards him, we will never connect with him. Instead, we need to be kind, tenderhearted and forgiving towards our husband. This will draw us closer together.

In this section I'm going to give you some suggestions for how you can **connect** with your husband and not **neglect** him.

Share experiences

A long time ago I watched a marriage video[19] where the speaker said that one of the best things a family can do is go camping. His reason was because something always goes wrong while camping (e.g. the car gets bogged, it rains, you discover you forgot to pack pillows) and the shared experience of having to deal with and overcome that problem creates closeness and great memories.

I think there's something in that!

I don't think you have to go camping or have a disaster to grow closer to your husband, though. I think sharing *good* experiences can be just as beneficial.

A friend of mine has a husband who loves surfing. It's his passion. After years of being married to him she decided to get some surfing lessons. She discovered, to her surprise, that she loved it! She quickly bought a wet suit and surf board and they began going surfing together. I saw them at a party about a month after she'd started surfing. I asked her how she was enjoying it and she enthusiastically began telling me about it. I then turned to her husband and said, "You must be *loving* it that she's surfing with you." I will never forget the look of absolute joy in his eyes when he said, "Oh yeah!" His whole face was lit up. He said he was so excited that now they could surf together, they could go on surfing holidays as a family and they could talk about surfing together. She had suddenly (and happily) joined his world. We should never underestimate what it means to our husbands to share their passions.

---

19 Nope, sorry, I can't reference it, I have no idea what it was called!

CONNECT

109

Part of sharing experiences is finding new leisure activities in common, like I discussed at the start of this section. To be clear, this doesn't mean that you should try to get your husband to like your hobbies! You definitely shouldn't stress or get annoyed if your husband refuses to be interested in the things you like doing. Accept it, get over it and find some girlfriends who will share your interests. (Although, as a side point, you should try to limit the time you spend on your hobbies if you're a bit 'obsessed' with them, otherwise it will draw you away from your husband.)

Instead, what you can do is give his interests a try.

By this I mean a proper try. Not, "Oh, I tried that once and I didn't like it", but you should actually really make an effort. Ask God to help you! If he loves a particular sport, ask him to teach you about the rules and the teams, and go along to at least a couple of the games. If he loves fishing, get him to take you out fishing a few times and learn about the different techniques. If he loves gardening, ask him how you can help and try to learn about the different plants and how to look after them.

If you've given it a real try and you still don't enjoy doing it, that's okay. You shouldn't pretend to love something you don't—it's just not sustainable. But at least you'll be able to appreciate the good or bad news associated with his interest. For example, I think cricket has to be the most boring sport in the world, especially five day test matches. Josh thinks they are brilliant. So, I knew it was important to learn how to score, how to get out, who the main Australian players are and what are good and bad scores. I tried going to a couple of games and watching it a bit with him but I seriously could not keep my mind focussed on it. It's so boring! But, because I understand how the game is played, when he says to me: "I can't believe Australia are 22/3",

I can say: "Are you serious? That's terrible! Who's out?" which is far nicer than "Who cares?!"

And if you really can't enjoy anything your husband loves, I strongly encourage you to make the effort to find some interests that you both like. Suggest to him that you both try something new (only if he wants to, though!).

Finally, I've learnt that when your husband says, "Look at this" or "Can you come here?" you should go *straight* away. He wants to share an experience with you. That's fantastic: he picked *you*, not someone else, and this is how you can create memories together. Okay, so you might have been the only available person, but if you whinge and drag your heels, he may not ask you next time, thinking that you don't care. This just creates separateness, not closeness. And wouldn't you love him to come straight away if you wanted to share an experience with him?

Ask about his work

At church or social events if I'm introduced to a man one of the first things I ask him about is his work. This is mainly because I find it the easiest thing to converse with a guy about. Unless he hates his job, a man can usually talk for a long time about what he does. If his wife is standing next to him it's not unusual for her, when she hears his responses to my questions, to say, "I didn't know that!"

I'm not asking particularly insightful questions, just things like what he does, how he does what he does and whether he enjoys it. They are probably exactly the same questions his wife asked when they first met. However, since getting married she probably stopped asking about her husband's work. She found it too difficult to understand, or more likely, too boring.

However, asking your husband about his work is a great way to connect with him. I'm not suggesting you bombard him with questions every day, but over the weeks and months ask him a range of questions to find out what he does, who he does it with and whether he likes it. For example, it's good to find out:

- The main tasks or projects he's working on
- Why those tasks or projects are important
- What the major steps are that he needs to take to complete those tasks or projects
- What he likes most about his job
- What he likes least about his job
- Who he likes working with and why

- Who he dislikes working with and why

- What his career aspirations are, if any

Men attach a lot of importance to their work so if your husband is able to share with you his successes and his challenges it will make him feel more connected to you. It will also give you an opportunity to show your respect for his abilities and to understand more clearly how he is feeling.

Unselfishness is needed

Marriage is a strange thing. No-one marries someone for unselfish reasons. We marry because we think it will be good for us and because it will give us what we want, such as friendship, love, companionship, children and financial security.

But *once* you get married, you need to be unselfish to make it work. You can't be thinking about what you get from the marriage, but what you can give to the marriage. It's not about what he does for you but about what you do for him.

If you want to live a selfish life (that is, do what you want, when you want, how you want), *don't get married.* I say that because a good marriage is all about being unselfish. It's about putting his needs before your own, blessing him and doing nice things for him. It's always an effort to do something nice for someone else, yet we love it when someone does it for us! Therefore, we should do it for our husbands.

I find it challenging to consistently be unselfish and do nice things for Josh. And when I am doing something nice for him I sometimes complain about doing it, which basically defeats the purpose!

Matthew 5:43-48 talks about loving your enemies. It starts off by saying: "You have heard the law that says, 'Love your neighbour' and hate your enemy." In marriage we can have this same mentality: if my husband treats me well (like a neighbour), I will be nice to him. But if he's nasty (like an enemy), then I have the right to be nasty as well. Jesus, however, goes on to teach that not only should we refrain from being mean to those who have wronged us, we should actually love them. Luke recorded Jesus' words as follows:

"...love your enemies! Do good to those who hate you. Bless those who curse you. Pray for those who hurt you."

Luke 6:27b-28

This Scripture is clear. We are to love, pray for, bless and do good to our enemies. If Jesus says we should do this for our enemies, how much more should we love, pray for, bless and do good to our husbands whom we promised to love and honour?

And there's more. Jesus goes on to say:

"If someone slaps you on one cheek, offer the other cheek also. If someone demands your coat, offer your shirt also. Give to anyone who asks; and when things are taken away from you, don't try to get them back. Do to others as you would like them to do to you."

Luke 6:29-31

In other words, when someone asks us to do something for them that we don't want to do, we should not only do it, but give them more than they ask.

So, if your husband asks you to do something you don't like doing, such as iron his shirt, instead of arguing, saying no or complaining, iron his shirt and then iron his jeans as well. If he asks you to make him dinner, make him dessert as well. If he asks you to give him a massage, give him a back scratch as well. This puts the 'power' back in your hands. Instead of giving begrudgingly or out of obedience, you are giving by choice and out of love. When you have chosen to 'go the extra mile' it is amazing how much better you feel about doing something you didn't want to do.

Because this is an area I struggle with, every now and then I challenge myself to do a certain number of nice things for Josh each day. Normally it's something like five nice things on a weekday and ten nice things on a weekend day. Nice things can include making him lunch, putting away his clothes, making tea, doing the dishes, giving him a back rub, making him a cup of tea or doing the grocery shopping. Even if these things are my 'normal' household jobs, they are still nice things I am doing for him, because I'm saving him from having to do them. Whenever I set this challenge it's interesting how much happier I am to do the tasks I dislike (like ironing) because I'm thinking, "Good, that brings me up to six nice things for the day...now if I make him a cup of tea, give him a back rub, make dinner and do the dishes, that will be my ten things done!" My whole perspective changes from one of whinging about doing things to eagerly looking for opportunities to bless him. Being loving in this way helps me connect with him, rather than resent him.

I don't do it all the time, just when I think I'm getting slack in being nice to him because it helps remind me of the need to be less selfish. I challenge you to give it a try!

Forgive even if he doesn't say sorry

You will have plenty of opportunities to practice forgiveness in marriage.

Your husband will hurt you in many ways. He might be inconsiderate or selfish. He might be unfair or mean. He might be unkind or rude. He might also make mistakes like crashing the car, breaking your grandmother's tea set or making a bad financial decision.

Our natural reaction is to get angry, cry, say something hurtful or withdraw. Many people would say this reaction is completely justifiable.

The Bible, however, teaches us something completely different.

> Make allowance for each other's faults, and forgive anyone who offends you. Remember, the Lord forgave you, so you must forgive others.

Colossians 3:13

We need to forgive our husbands for several reasons. Firstly, we forgive because God forgave us, and continues to forgive us. Secondly, the Bible teaches in Mark 11:25 that we need to forgive so God can forgive us. If we don't forgive, it separates us from God. Thirdly, we should forgive because unforgiveness causes us more pain in the long-term. Unforgiveness hurts us, causing us to become bitter, twisted and angry. Finally, if we don't forgive, the connection between us and our husbands will be broken. Forgiveness will restore that connection.

CONNECT

Forgiveness, however, is very hard. Especially when your husband has hurt you deeply. I have found that forgiveness is a process, one that I need God to help me with every step of the way. I've outlined the process I go through below in the hope that it might help you too:

1. **Tell God how irritated, frustrated, angry and hurt you are**

   It is unhealthy to hold in your feelings of anger and hurt, but venting to other people is usually a bad idea. As I explained earlier, God is the best person to vent to, *always*. I usually to go into another room, shut the door and then yell/cry/scream to God (preferably under my breath so Josh can't hear), telling Him exactly how upset I am with Josh. The great thing is that God always lets me get it off my chest before He begins to gently remind me of what I should do.

2. **Thank God for forgiving you**

   It's good to remember that God forgave you for all your sins. Thank Him for forgiving you. It will put you in a more gracious frame of mind!

3. **Ask God to show you if you've done anything wrong in the situation**

   Sometimes we can be so pre-occupied with the hurt that we forget our part in the matter. Sometimes you will be completely innocent, but sometimes you will have done something wrong as well. If so, you should ask God for forgiveness for your part and tell the person you are sorry for what you did wrong[20]. Again, this will help you adjust your attitude!

---

20 See *Apologise well* for advice on apologising.

THAT BOOK FOR WIVES

4. Ask God to help you forgive your husband

If you don't feel like forgiving, I suggest asking God first to give you the desire to forgive. Once He gives you the desire to forgive (and He will if you ask Him), then ask God to help you to forgive.

5. Forgive your husband

Once God has given you the desire to forgive, it is really helpful to say out loud, "I forgive him for *[whatever his offence is]*", even if you don't mean it just yet. There is power in speaking the words out loud! Keep saying it until you really mean it.

6. Apply Luke 6:27-28

Luke 6:27-28 gives a great model for responding to someone who has hurt us:

- Love them
- Do good things for them
- Bless them
- Pray for them

I find that this works well if you apply it in reverse: if you *pray* for your husband, pray God's *blessing* on him and then *do something nice* for him, you will start feeling and being more *loving* towards him again! It also really helps to 'cement' your forgiveness.

7. Tell your husband that you forgive him (maybe)

Once you have genuinely forgiven your husband, what should you do?

Well, if your husband is aware that you're upset with him, you should say, "I forgive you" to him. Be careful, though, not to follow your forgiveness with the word "but". Saying, "I forgive you *but* you really hurt me", "I forgive you *but* I'm so angry that you..." or "I forgive you *but* don't ever do that again" is not really true forgiveness. Just say, "I forgive you" and leave it at that. Also, please don't just say, "It's okay", because it's *not* okay. He has done the wrong thing. Instead, say the incredibly powerful words, "I forgive you". That's what he wants and needs to hear.

If however, your husband doesn't know that he has offended you I suggest you don't say anything. If you've forgiven him, there is no need to make him feel bad by telling him what he did wrong. This is especially the case when it is something minor that is unlikely to be repeated.

8. Repeat steps 5 and 6 as needed

After you've forgiven him you might find you feel that hurt again later. Sometimes I've thought I've forgiven only to discover that I still feel hurt, bitter or resentful when I've remembered the incident later. Sometimes it's only been days later—sometimes it's even been months. The key is to forgive him every time you remember the hurt (go through steps 5 and 6 again). You may remember many times but each time the hurt should be less and the forgiveness should be quicker. Keep in mind that forgiveness is a process.

The forgiveness process should take place without your husband being aware of it. It's probably not very helpful to tell him that you've been trying to forgive him but can't! However, if he knows he has really hurt you and can tell that you're upset, it is a good idea to say: "I'm hurt right now and I need some time to pray about it. I will come and talk to you about it when I've processed what's happened." This is much better than the silent treatment. It lets him know that while you're upset, you are actively doing something to deal with it and that you will talk with him about it when you're ready.

I'm anticipating four arguments to this process of forgiveness:

1. But he doesn't deserve my forgiveness

No-one deserves forgiveness. The Bible says:

> For everyone has sinned; we all fall short of God's glorious standard.
> **Romans 3:23**

Not one of us will ever do enough good in our lives to make up for all the bad we have done. We all deserve eternal punishment from God. But the good news is that the Bible goes on to say:

> Yet God, in his grace, freely makes us right in his sight. He did this through Christ Jesus when he freed us from the penalty for our sins. For God presented Jesus as the sacrifice for sin. People are made right with God when they believe that Jesus sacrificed his life, shedding his blood.
> **Romans 3:24-25b**

Even though we didn't deserve it, God sent His only son Jesus to take our punishment for sin. And now God offers everyone, regardless of their sins, forgiveness through his sacrifice. God forgives us, not because we deserve it, but because He is good and gracious and kind.

If we have accepted God's forgiveness, we also ought to forgive our husband, whether he deserves it or not, just as we want God (and our husband) to forgive us when we don't deserve it either.

2. But he didn't say sorry

Often your husband may not be aware that he's done anything wrong, or if he is aware, he thinks it's your fault anyway (which, by the way, may be true!). Even if he knows it's his own fault he may refuse to say sorry—many people find this hard to do, either due to their upbringing or their personality (Cholerics find it very, very hard to say sorry[21]).

Either way, just because someone hasn't said sorry is no excuse for not forgiving. Forgiveness is not about him. Like I said earlier, unforgiveness will make you bitter, slowly destroying you and your marriage. Jesus died for us before we said sorry. We need to be willing to forgive even if our husbands never acknowledge their guilt.

3. But if I forgive he just gets away with it

Sometimes we refuse to forgive because we think that if we do forgive our husband he will never learn. We want to make him suffer for hurting us. We think not forgiving him will punish him. But actually it just punishes us. We are the ones who suffer from the anger and bitterness.

We need to trust that God will, in His time, convict and deal with our husband. And besides, didn't we 'just get away with it' when Jesus forgave us, washed us clean and gave us a new life? The story of the unforgiving servant in Matthew 18:21-35 is very relevant here.

---

21 *Personality Plus*, Florence Littauer, 1983, Revell, pp. 128-129

4. But then he'll probably do it again

Probably. He's human, after all. Just like you keep making the same mistakes over and over. You need to ask God to give you more grace and mercy towards him. If you really feel the need to talk to him about what he's done so he's aware, I suggest you follow the process I outlined earlier. That is, tell him once (nicely) and then if he hasn't changed after a suitable interval, remind him once more. After that, you might as well just accept that this is the way he is and leave him in God's hands to sort out[22].

I'm not suggesting this is easy. But without forgiveness you can't have a healthy marriage. Forgiveness keeps your connection strong.

---

22 Please note: if your husband has done something really destructive (e.g. cheated on you, abused you) you will need to get additional counsel about putting boundaries in place to prevent him being able to hurt you again. You will still need to ask God's help to forgive him so that you don't get bitter, but you will also need some godly advice about keeping safe.

Apologise well

Of course you will hurt your husband in many ways too. You might be inconsiderate, selfish, unfair, mean, unkind or rude. You might make mistakes like crashing the car, breaking his phone or nearly burning the house down because you forgot you had food cooking on the stove[23].

When you've done the wrong thing, apologise.

However, before you apologise, it's a good idea to pray. Ask God to help you understand exactly what mistakes you made that resulted in you hurting your husband (e.g. not paying attention, not showing respect for his possessions, trying to do too many things at the same time). Understanding your mistake will help you genuinely apologise and help prevent you from making the same mistake again. You should also ask God to forgive you for what you did wrong and ask Him to help you change.

Then, you need to apologise properly to your husband. An off-hand "sorry" straight after you've hurt him is not going to be good enough. Instead:

- Look him in the eye when you say you're sorry. This way he can see you are being genuine.

- Be specific about what you did wrong. For example, "I'm so sorry I was selfish when I told our friends we wouldn't go out to dinner with them. I was only thinking about what was easiest for me and not about what you would like".

---

23 I may be talking from experience here...

Note: if you can't really understand what he's getting so worked up about, you need some prayer and genuine soul-searching to identify exactly what you did wrong. Reconciliation can't really come until you can identify your mistake.

- Never say, "I'm sorry, but...". Don't ruin the apology by using it as an opportunity to tell him what he did wrong or to lay the blame back on him. If he is partly to blame or has also done something wrong, that is for him to deal with. All you can do is focus on what you can change, that is, what you did wrong.

- Tell your husband how you plan to change and how, with God's help, you could do things differently in the future. For example: "Next time I'll ask you first what you'd like to do, before I give an answer". This shows genuine repentance.

I believe you should apologise like this even if it's mostly your husband's fault! Even if your husband is 95% to blame and you are only 5% to blame, you should ask God to show you your wrong (maybe your attitude or your reaction) and then genuinely apologise for that. Sometimes when you apologise it will 'inspire' your husband to also apologise for his part. But not always. Getting him to apologise is not the aim here. The aim is to make sure that *your* heart is right before God and that *you* have made peace with your husband.

Arguments should be interesting

Josh and I started arguing the minute we met and nearly 20 years later we haven't stopped. Usually we enjoy arguing, especially when it's the spirited type of argument that sharpens your mind and forces you to think clearly. It's fun and I think it's part of the reason we're attracted to each other.

However, a lot of arguments in marriages are not like this! When arguing is nasty, mean, cruel or domineering it is wrong. When you try to force your point of view, when you bring up 'forgiven' issues from the past, or when you stubbornly demand your way, it is not good.

If you are arguing about a decision that needs to be made for you as a couple or family, then it's important that you submit[24]. This will resolve the argument immediately.

However, if you're arguing about opinions rather than decisions, you do not have to agree with everything your husband says. It can be good and fun to argue about issues where you have different opinions as it can help you learn from each other. But when you disagree about serious issues that may impact your life, you need to be very careful.

Firstly, you need to decide whether it is worth discussing. Don't argue about something petty or irrelevant. It is not necessary to agree (or argue!) about everything in life.

---

24 See *Submission is great* for an explanation of submission.

Secondly, if it is something worth discussing, consi
your 'rules of engagement'. Don't ever bring up the pas
or be nasty and mean. Don't argue in front of other people,
especially your kids. Don't attack them as a person. Don't
physically hurt them. Don't give them the silent treatment
which makes finding a resolution impossible.

Remember, you're probably never going to 'win' an
argument. Neither of you are likely to ever say: "Oh, well,
when you put it like that, you're totally right" [25]. Significant
differences in point of view may never be resolved. But
it's important that the argument ends with peace not
nastiness. When you do have a different point of view I
encourage you to pray about it, even if you're convinced
your view is right. God will give you wisdom about whether
to leave the discussion for now or whether maybe you need
to change your viewpoint!

---

25 In saying that, though, we had an argument recently about how a
situation should be handled. It was to do with someone else, so it wasn't
a submission issue. I was very firm on my point of view, as was Josh.
He listened to all of my arguments, then responded to each one (he was
being far more gracious than I was, I might add) and by the end I literally
went: "Oh, I see where you are coming from. That makes sense. Actually,
I think you're right!" Of course, not all our arguments end that easily,
though, as I can be pretty stubborn!

ce is better than sleep

...ible says:

> "Don't let the sun go down while you are still angry."
> **Ephesians 4:26**

This is such good advice! Before we got married, Josh and I were encouraged to embrace this principle. We thought it was a good idea, and agreed to have a rule that we can't go to sleep if we're mad at each other.

I have found this to be a very irritating rule when one of us starts a fight (never intentionally, of course) just before we are about to go to sleep after a long and tiring day. As irritating as it is, however, it is better to sacrifice some sleep in order to have peace restored in your relationship.

Imagine what will happen if you go to sleep mad with each other:

1. You will sleep on opposite sides of the bed, facing away from each other, not touching. Any accidental touch will probably elicit a cranky response.

2. You won't talk in the morning. You will be too angry and in too much of a hurry.

3. All day long you'll stew on the argument and you'll be angry or tense.

4. You'll get home, tired from the day and will probably argue again or be so annoyed that you give each other the silent treatment. Even worse, you're likely to withhold sex from each other.

THAT BOOK FOR WIVES

This can go on for days! And the longer it is left, th
it is to fix.

The solution is simple: don't go to sleep angry with each other. I used to think this meant you had to have resolved the issue before you went to sleep. This is neither realistic nor necessary, especially since some issues take a long time to work through and late at night is not usually the best time to do this. Instead, what you need to do is create peace—that is, get to a point where you can touch your husband lovingly and say, "I love you" (and mean it) and agree to talk about it more the next day.

It can take time to change your attitude from one of anger to one of peace so it might be tempting to go to sleep and leave it for tomorrow, especially if you're really tired. But trust me, making peace will save you sleep anyway—there's nothing like stewing over an argument to keep you awake!

Simple choices like this can ensure that whenever your relationship is broken through an argument the connection is restored before the day is over.

You might be wondering what you can do if he doesn't agree to this. What if he refuses to have a 'don't go to sleep angry' rule? What if he refuses to acknowledge your attempts to make peace?

Well, the Bible also says:

> "Do all that you can to live in peace with everyone."
> **Romans 12:18**

The important thing is that you make a personal decision to never go to sleep angry with your husband. Forgive him (this will probably require you to pray silently, talking through your frustrations with God first so you can get to a place of genuine forgiveness) and then, if he's still awake, apologise to him for your anger. He may not reply but at least you have done all that you can to be at peace. When you wake up in the morning, be respectful and loving. It is very difficult for one person to continue an argument by themselves!

Friendship is better than sleep

I don't get as much sleep as I'd like. Ever since Year 12, when I set myself a bed-time of 10.30pm, I've always felt that 10.30pm was the right time to turn off the light and go to sleep. Any later and I start getting grumpy.

However, I married a night owl. This really threw me for the first five or so years of marriage. I'd come home from work eager to tell Josh about my day and would then proceed to do so while I followed him around the garden as he watered, or while sitting on the edge of his couch as he watched the news. I found it curious and somewhat irritating that he didn't seem all that interested in what I had to say. And when I asked him about his day I'd get a non-committal "good" or "fine"... just like he was a teenage boy and I was his mother!

He'd be like this until around 7.00pm, then he'd slowly start to fill me in on his day. Even huge, huge news was unlikely to surface before then. By around 10.00pm he'd have warmed up and be ready to talk and talk and talk, whereas I'd be tired and wanting to go to sleep. By 10.30pm (my bed-time!) I'd say: "I need to sleep!" and grumpily try to ignore him. He'd usually persist in talking and I'd either be interested in spite of myself, or get grumpier and grumpier, knowing it was now 10.45pm and I'd missed 15 minutes of sleep!

So the end result was that I was not getting much sleep, I got grumpy at my husband every night for wanting to talk to me, and I missed out on hearing my husband's thoughts, dreams and plans.

Thankfully, one day I realised that half an hour or even an hour less sleep a day was worth it to have a husband who wanted to talk to me! Here I was complaining about my husband wanting to talk to me when so many women were telling me they struggled to get even a few sentences out of their men! I started to see those late night talks in bed as a huge blessing and as a wonderful opportunity to truly be my husband's best friend. I have friends who are jealous of what I have because their husbands think beds are only for two things (and "talkin' ain't one of them"!).

So, I don't get as much sleep as I'd like. In fact, my normal bed-time is now around midnight and often much later, *but* I get to talk with my husband for at least half an hour, usually an hour, every single night. It makes us both happy and now I look forward to it as a time when I can talk about my day too. Besides, it made me consider my usual start time at work and I discovered that the world didn't fall apart if I started half an hour later![26]

26 Clearly I wrote this part before having kids, back when I could choose what time I got up! Still, the fact I have very late nights meant that when my kids were babies I was insistent on the first morning feed not being before 6.30am and I always tried to push it to at least 7.00am. Now they usually get up around 7.00am—7.30am which means it's always a mad rush to get ready for school, but it's worth it for that extra half an hour of sleep!

He has different talking times

As I've just explained, it took me a while to realise that the best time to talk with Josh is late at night. Before I figured this out, I used to get very frustrated with him for not listening to me when I was talking to him. I'd try to tell him about something and only get an "Uh huh" kind of answer. As I'd wait for an answer I could see that one part of his brain had heard me and was telling another part of his brain that someone had said something and that he should make some sort of response. And sometimes that other part of his brain would be unsuccessful in communicating with the tongue and I wouldn't get any answer at all! I used to get very cranky when this happened. I felt it was very rude and unloving that my husband didn't want to genuinely listen and respond to what I wanted to tell him.

But Josh *is* a good listener and does like to talk with me. My problem was that I was picking all the wrong times to talk with him.

Finally I realised that right after work was not a good time for him. After spending a whole day talking with people at work he was tired. When he got home all he wanted was a chance to unwind, which he usually did by watering the garden. Telling him all about my day while I followed him around as he watered was interrupting his much needed wind-down time. I didn't understand this because I used to unwind by reading a book for half an hour on the bus after work. This meant that by the time I got home I was ready to talk!

I also realised that talking with him while he was watching TV was a bad idea too. At first I thought it was okay to talk with him if he was only watching the news or sport since they were so boring anyway. I didn't grasp the idea that he could possibly find them interesting. Once I realised that obviously he did find them interesting (or he wouldn't watch them!) it made sense. I didn't like it when he'd talk to me while I was watching TV either. One time, when I was watching the movie *Nanny McPhee*, he came downstairs right at the end and started asking me questions about the movie. In response to his: "Why is her tooth like that?" I crossly answered, "It just is!" (In other words: "Shut up, I'm trying to watch this very sweet ending")[27].

It's really not hard to figure out the best times to talk with your husband. Just notice when he gives you short or non-existent responses (bad time) and when he is the one doing all the talking (good time). It's just a matter of accepting that everyone has different times. If you can understand this you will increase your connection with your husband considerably—you won't be annoying him by talking to him when he's distracted and you'll be listening when he's ready to communicate. And he's far more likely to listen to you then too!

---

27 By the way, I felt very guilty when I realised how rude I was to Josh in the Nanny McPhee incident. I really should not have got cranky with him—just like I don't want him to get cranky with me if I talk to him while he's watching something. I should have just paused the movie and answered his questions! By not wanting to talk to him, I was telling him that watching the movie was more important to me than communicating with him. I want to make sure he knows he's more important to me than some movie.

Listening is a skill worth learning

Talking at your husband is not enough to connect—we need to listen to what he has to say too! The Bible tells us we need to be quick to listen and slow to speak.

> "You must all be quick to listen, slow to speak, and slow to get angry."
> **James 1:19**

Unfortunately I tend to get this around the wrong way. I'm very quick to talk (no-one will deny my ability to talk!) which unfortunately means I'm not all that quick to listen.

Years ago when I was studying Adult Education I read a very confronting quiz about listening skills. It asked questions like: "When in a conversation with someone, are you busy thinking about what you're going to say next, rather than actually listening to them?" and "Do you get impatient with slow speakers and try to finish their sentence for them?". I had to answer "Yes"! This made me realise that I had some ways to go if I wanted to be a wife who really listened to her husband.

Thankfully, the subject also provided some great information about active listening. When I remember to use these skills I am definitely a far better listener! I have summarised this information in the following table[28]:

---

28 Adapted from *People Skills*, R. Bolton, 1986, Prentice Hall Australia, p. 30

Skill Sets	Behaviours	Hints
Attending Skills *(Physically showing that you're listening)*	Have a posture of involvement	• Lean forward • Have 'open' body language • Respect personal space
	Use appropriate body motion	• Avoid distracting motions and gestures • Move body in response to the speaker
	Use appropriate eye contact	• Focus softly on the speaker's face/ eyes • Occasionally shift gaze to other parts of their body (e.g. to their hand when they gesture)
	Create a non-distracting environment	• Cut distractions to a minimum • Remove sizeable barriers
Following Skills *(How you should behave while listening)*	Only have minimal encouragers	• Restrict talking to small encouragers like "Really?" or "Oh!" • Don't interrupt or finish their sentences
	Only ask infrequent questions	• Don't ask too many questions • Use open questions • Only ask one question at a time
	Be silent and attentive	• Don't allow your attention to wander • Think about what the speaker is saying (not about how you want to respond)
Reflecting Skills *(Ensuring the message sent is the message received)*	Paraphrase	• Be concise • Use your own words • Paraphrase only the essence of the speaker's content
	Summarise	• Briefly restate the speaker's main themes and feelings • Help the speaker better understand the key issues

It sounds pretty basic, but actually applying these skills takes effort.

When your husband is trying to tell you something, active listening means stopping what you're doing, turning to face him, not interrupting him and paying attention to what he's saying. A simple paraphrase at the end to show him you've understood what he's saying is also powerful (For example: "You must be so frustrated that your boss is not listening to your ideas that will make the team work better").

Allan Pease[29], has another great technique for being a good listener. He suggests nodding and waiting five seconds after the speaker has stopped talking as the speaker will usually recommence talking in that time. After learning this technique I decided to (surreptitiously!) try this out on a quiet friend of mine. She started to tell me about something that was upsetting her. Instead of jumping in with sympathy and advice whenever she paused like I usually would, I tried nodding and waiting five seconds. Each time (even though I thought she was finished), she started talking again. My 'quiet' friend ended up talking for about 20 minutes with me only adding the odd "Oh no" or "Really?" or "How frustrating!" It made me realise that maybe she wasn't quiet after all—I just never gave her a chance to speak! If your husband isn't much of a talker, or even if he is, I encourage you to give this technique a try.

Listening, really listening, will most likely make your husband want to talk to you more. And the more he talks to you, the more you'll understand and be able to connect with him.

----

29 *Questions are the Answers: How to get to 'Yes' in Network Marketing*, Allan Pease, 2000, Pease International Pty Ltd, p. 51

CONNECT

Subtle hints don't work

Wives can be great at throwing out subtle hints like: "(Sigh) Sarah got flowers today; she's so lucky" or "I really wish I had one of those latest phones". Or, when it gets close to our birthday, we might leave catalogues around the house with our desired objects circled. Then we get disappointed or even angry when our insensitive husbands don't pick up on our hints and instead buy us a vacuum cleaner![30]

I've learnt that it is really unfair to make our husbands guess or interpret our hints. I know it's not romantic, but I think it's just better to come right out and say: "For my birthday I'd like either A, B or C". This way your husband isn't frantically trying to read your mind to find out what you want and he also has some options to choose from so there is a bit of a surprise.

We send such mixed messages anyway. One of our friends once told me how his wife had seen a pet in a shop window and then had gone on and on about how cute it was, how well it would fit in with their other pets and how it would probably be put down if no-one bought it. So when she wasn't looking he went back and bought it for her. Then she got angry at him for wasting money on a pet! I would have read the situation the same way he did, but she insists she was just joking around. And with the 'vacuum cleaner as a birthday present' scenario above I have to admit I had mentioned several times that I wanted that particular vacuum cleaner!

Don't set your husband up for failure. Tell him clearly what you'd like. This way you will both be happy.

---

30 Again, I may be talking from experience here ☺

What if you give him a list of reasonable options and he still gives you something you don't want? I suggest you get some perspective. There are so many people who are too poor to get any presents at all. Be grateful for what you get. You are blessed even if you get rubbish presents—at least he cared enough to get you something!

And, if you have a husband who doesn't do presents at all, I encourage you to pray and ask God to help you understand your husband more. It doesn't mean he doesn't love you or care about you—it's just clearly not his love language. Choose to accept that he won't give you a present, *ever*, and look for other things to enjoy about your birthday such as dinner with him or your family.

You shouldn't expect your husband to remember your birthday and wedding anniversary either. Be kind and remind! I'm blessed with a husband who always remembers dates, but I'm hopeless with remembering everyone else's birthdays. I know how much I appreciate it when people say things like, "I can't believe I'll be 30 soon" or "I'm trying to work out if I'm going to do anything for my birthday next Saturday" or something like that. I never feel sorry for people who don't tell anyone it's their birthday then get depressed because no-one wishes them happy birthday. Nobody is as interested in your birthday as you are. I know we'd like our husbands to care enough to remember, but it's unlikely to be a lack of care that makes him forget, he's probably just busy or tired. Be nice and remind him.

What if you remind him and he still forgets? Well, if he hasn't said, "Happy Birthday" by the time breakfast is over, maybe you can remind him in a gentle, non-judgemental way by saying something like, "I can't believe I'm xx years old now!" You never know, he may have been pretending not to remember because he has a surprise planned for you. And, if not, you've given him a chance to say, "Oh, that's right, Happy Birthday honey!" and he'll also then have the chance to go buy you something before the day is over.

Let your actions build trust

You should never keep secrets from your husband[31]. Secrets about *anything* lead to lies and a loss of trust. They are so destructive. You need to avoid keeping any type of secret from your husband, no matter how hard it is to tell the truth.

If you tell him the truth you will never be afraid of him finding out. If you broke his tool, spent way too much on clothes, said something bad about him to someone else, told one of his secrets to someone else—whatever it is, confess your sin! Tell him. Tell him now. Don't wait. Well... maybe wait until a good time (i.e. not when he's just got home from work), but make sure you deal with it today, before you go to sleep. It is so much better to deal with the consequences now than to wait until later. The longer you wait, the harder it is to confess and the worse you'll feel. If it's something you did a year ago, three years ago, ten years ago—tell him today. Do it now. Secrets kill connection and trust. Don't excuse your behaviour. Tell him what you did wrong and why you did it, apologise genuinely and accept responsibility. By confessing you can deal with the issue and you can move forward in your marriage. You need to do whatever you can to build, not destroy, trust.

In relation to money I believe that you should have complete openness with your husband. You should never lie about what you have spent your money on. If you want to make a significant purchase it's always wise to discuss it with

---

31 Surprises (where you will tell them the truth very soon) are fine, secrets (where you don't ever want them to know the truth) are not.

your husband first. That way you can find out if he has any concerns or issues with it first. This might seem unfair, especially if you're working as well, but part of marriage is agreeing to share all that you have, including your money. Consequently, you should submit to your husband's decision when you want to buy something.

Talk to your husband about what he thinks is reasonable for you to just buy and what he'd rather you run past him first. If I'm needing/wanting something small like a top or a pair of jeans, I just buy it. But if I want to go on a big clothes shopping spree I'll discuss with Josh first how much to spend. He usually suggests a very generous figure, often much more than I was planning to spend[32]. I love this because it gives me a boundary within which I am free to buy as much as I want. It helps me keep controlled (only buying what I really want or need) and I have no fear of going home that night and showing him my purchases!

A final thought about trust. Be careful about any secrets your husband tells you. You want your husband to be able to trust you completely, but he can't if you always tell your girlfriends/mum/sister what he says. Make sure he can be confident you'll never break his trust. And if you do end up telling someone—don't ask your girlfriends/mum/sister not to give you away, instead, tell your husband what you did! Better to get it over and done with than worry about whether your girlfriends/mum/sister will accidentally slip up one day!

---

32 I realise not all husbands are generous when it comes to money. Some are very stingy. Again, I would encourage you to pray, asking God to give your husband (and you!) wisdom about your finances. God may touch your husband's heart, encouraging him to be generous with you, but more likely, God will change your heart, by helping you appreciate what you already have and by helping you understand why your husband is not wanting you to spend more.

Have other friends

It is healthy for both you and your husband to have other friends. I'm not saying you should spend excessive amounts of time with these other friends, but it's good for you to hang out with the girls and for him to hang out with the boys.

If your husband wants to watch sport at a friend's house or go fishing with the guys, encourage him to do so. It's good for him. And if he comes home two hours later than you expected, don't get angry at him (especially if his mates are there as it will make him look bad in front of his friends). Be glad for him that he was having fun with his friends.

It's good for you to hang out with your girlfriends as well. It's a chance for you to do some 'girly' things that your husband doesn't like doing. You shouldn't be spending so much time with your friends that your husband starts to feel neglected, but once every few weeks is good.

It's also good for both of you to regularly hang out with other couples, especially other Christian couples who can be an encouragement to you. However, this can be tricky as it's not always easy to find a couple with whom you both enjoy spending time. Be sensitive to your husband on this. If you are good friends with the wife but he doesn't connect with the husband, that's fine. Don't try to force dinner parties or visits on him, instead, just see the wife by yourself. But if your husband wants you to hang out with a couple where you don't get on that well with the wife, ask God to help you find points of connection so you can build a genuine friendship with her.

CONNECT

If you have couple friends then things like going out to dinner, going to the movies and going camping suddenly become more fun. Even though you are hanging out with other people, the fun you have together really does help you connect with your husband.

Put your kids third

Kids add a whole other element to your marriage.

Usually a screaming, vomiting, pooing element.

They are soooo time consuming. Simple tasks like leaving the house or eating dinner become a major event. Most parents of young children are so tired at the end of the day that it's hard to make time for each other.

Once you have kids your relationship will never be the same again. You just can't devote the same amount of time to each other. However, I don't believe that kids have to be the death of a good marriage. Instead, they can make it stronger. It all comes down to putting your kids third.

So many parents put their kids first. They make choices based on what will be best for the kids to the detriment of their marriage. This is unwise. Firstly because kids seriously do not need to be as spoiled as our society encourages. Secondly because one day they will grow up and leave home and have their own lives. When this happens you don't want to look at your husband and realise that you have nothing in common anymore.

Instead, God should always come first. That's just smart. Not only is He the Creator of the heavens and earth (and therefore worthy of all our praise and worship), He also loves us and helps us in every aspect of our lives. We need to make sure that each day we are taking the time to get to know Him through talking with Him and reading the Bible. The more we grow to know God and the more we grow to be like Him, the better mothers, wives and human beings we will be.

CONNECT

hen our husbands should come next. They are our partners for life. Unlike our children who we are only blessed with for their first 20 years or so, we will hopefully have 40, 50 or even 60 years with our husband. Our husbands should be the most important person after God in our lives, not just in our thoughts but in our actions.

When you have a baby, most husbands will understand that for those first couple of months everything is incredibly difficult simply due to a lack of sleep. During these months you will have to devote most of your time to feeding and caring for your baby. However, you can still make sure you show your husband that you appreciate him and care for him. He won't expect much, but you need to give him something. Include him, as much as he is willing, with the care of the baby. He might be happy to give the baby their bath each day or rock them so you can have a shower. Whatever you do, make sure you don't exclude him. Don't ever let it become just you and the baby, with your husband off to one side. Make sure it's the three of you together.

For example, I think it is wise to make sure your baby sleeps in a separate room from the very beginning[33]. If you don't, your husband may end up sleeping in a different room, which is hardly good for building your connection! Instead, make sure you are demonstrating to your husband (and your child) the importance of your relationship. You might argue that it's much easier for you to have the baby in with you so you can feed them in the night. I'm sure that's true, but if your husband has to go to work in the morning, I believe it's best for you to try to avoid waking

33 If your house is too small for your baby to have their own room, you can put your baby in your room for their day sleeps, and move them into the lounge room when you go to bed (a bassinet on wheels makes this easy). This way you are still keeping your bedroom as a special place for you and your husband.

him at night so he can have a good sleep. That may seem unfair when you're not getting sleep, but remember he has to go to work all day to earn money to help provide for you and the baby! You want him to be well rested so he can perform well at work and still have the energy to come home and help you with the baby in the evening. It's far better that you get up when the baby wakes, go out, shut your bedroom door and feed your baby in another room[34].

It is good for your kids to also see the romantic relationship between you and your husband. As they get older, let them see you kissing or holding hands. I regularly tell my kids how much I love Josh, how gorgeous he is and how I love kissing him. You don't have to go over the top, but it's good for your kids to know that you love each other and that the best kind of love is in a marriage, not in what they see on TV. Kids feel so much more secure if they know their parents love each other.

As the kids get older, another area to consider is your children's extra-curricular activities. Our society encourages allowing kids to explore all possible areas of talent, meaning kids can be taking dance, soccer, music, basketball and art lessons all in one week! Of course it's good to allow kids to exercise and have fun, but make sure doing so doesn't take up so much of the week that you never get to have quality time with your husband and kids. Think through any commitment to a Saturday sport, especially. Since Sundays you go to church (hopefully!), Saturdays may be the only day you have as a family together. I'm not saying you shouldn't let your kids do sport on a Saturday, only that you and your husband should really think through

---

34 If you had a multiple birth or a baby with medical issues, of course this scenario will be different. The point is to look for ways of maintaining and building your connection with your husband in those first few months as much as you can.

any regular commitment to make sure it won't become a drain on your family time.

If you can keep your kids at a healthy third place, you will continue to build connection with your husband as they grow up. Then your kids will actually help bring you closer together, because even though they create a lot of work, they also bring a huge amount of joy. And one day, when they leave home, instead of wondering how to talk to this husband of yours whom you barely know, you'll be busy planning your first empty-nester adventure! (I'm voting for a trip to Europe. ☺)

In-laws should be honoured

I am really blessed to have wonderful in-laws. My husband's parents are second parents to me and my sister-in-law and brother-in-law are fantastic too. I love my husband's family and I know that they love me.

So...I'm blessed. I've never had the in-law drama that so many other wives have. I've heard some really bad stories though, like the mother-in-law who literally hates the wife because she led her son to God; the mother-in-law who has a strange, dependant relationship with her son, who resents any other women in her son's life; the mother-in law who will only ring when she knows the wife will be out of the house; and the mother-in-law who visits for extended periods and expects the wife to wait on her, hand and foot!

These are really unpleasant situations. Sometimes the wife is totally innocent. She's done everything she can to be polite, respectful, friendly and considerate, and she has endured the unfair treatment with patience, forgiveness and a continuing desire for reconciliation.

Unfortunately, this isn't always the case. Sometimes, the wife resents her mother-in-law's relationship with her husband or dislikes the way her mother-in-law treats her husband.

The Bible says, "Do all that you can to live in peace with everyone" (Romans 12:18) and "Honour your father and your mother" (Exodus 20:12). While your in-laws are not your parents, they are your husband's parents so I believe

CONNECT

this command still applies. If you do not have a good relationship with your in-laws it will cause tension between you and your husband. If you have a good relationship with them, it will help strengthen your connection with your husband.

These pointers might help if you have a challenging relationship with your in-laws:

- Don't forget that your mother-in-law carried your husband for nine months, painfully gave birth to him, cleaned him, watched him while he slept and dreamed of great and wonderful things for him. She loves him intensely, possibly even more than you. She will probably be quicker to forgive him, slower to judge him and will always love him no matter what he does. It is no doubt very, very difficult for her to let go of someone who has consumed her life for at least 20 years. To see him loving another woman more than her would not be easy.

- You do not have to be best friends with your mother-in-law, but it's a good idea to try to find some common interests. Find something you can enjoy doing together and do it regularly. Make extra effort to be friendly and accommodating.

- Honour your in-laws. This means thinking about them respectfully, speaking to them respectfully and speaking about them respectfully whether they can hear you or not. Everyone is sensitive about their family and even if your husband says something negative about his family, don't join in with your own complaints about them. He will not like anything you say that is negative about them, even if it's true.

- Don't try to make your husband choose between pleasing you and pleasing his family. He will want to do both and this will be very difficult for him. Unless it is incredibly important to you, try to fit in with what his family wants. If it *is* something that is incredibly important to you, talk to your husband in terms of why it is important to you and do so in a way that shows you understand his family's perspective as well. Then submit and trust that God will guide your husband to make the best decision.

- When your in-laws visit, make every effort to make them feel welcome, loved, and at home. This can be tricky if your mother-in-law is constantly trying to tell you how to clean, cook or take care of your children. Pray that God gives you wisdom. Maybe your mother-in-law is right—she *has* been there and done that—and maybe you should listen to her advice. She's trying to help! And if she isn't right, God will help you know how to handle the situation. I believe that it's okay to tell her if you don't agree with her advice, but you need to do so in a polite and kind way which honours her. For example, "That's kind of you to give me some advice. I'm trying a different method at the moment but I will keep that in mind. Thank you."

- If your in-laws are really unpleasant I encourage you to ask God to help you forgive them and love them. As Jesus teaches, pray for them, bless them and do nice things for them. It will probably be worth memorising Luke 6:27-28[35] and saying it (in your mind!) whenever you think about them. And each time you are about to meet them, spend some time in prayer first thanking God for them and asking Him to help you speak words of life, encouragement and blessing to them.

---

35 "...love your enemies! Do good to those who hate you. Bless those who curse you. Pray for those who hurt you."

On the flipside, your husband may struggle with the relationship you have with your parents, especially if you are quite close. If you are close to your parents it is important that you do as Genesis 2:24 says and 'leave' your parents when you marry your husband. As a child my mother was my best friend and while I am still really close to her, I had to make it clear to Josh when we got married that he came first and that he was now my 'best' friend. At all times, my first allegiance should be to him, not my mum. While this was hard for me, my mum was really good about it. She knew the importance of me relying on Josh more than her. Of course, I still regularly seek my mum for advice and wisdom and I really appreciate her friendship, but my husband has to have no doubt that he comes first.

Remember the good times

Keeping a journal is a great habit. I go through times of being more or less diligent with this, but when I read one of my old entries a while ago it reminded me of how blessed I am to have Josh. I had totally forgotten the following incident until I re-read it in my journal. Because it shows what a great husband he is, I can't resist putting in an extract, even if it does highlight how clumsy I am.

Thank you Lord for keeping me safe last night when I fell off the bus. It was so embarrassing, but I could have been hurt much worse. Thank you for the kindness of the bus driver in helping me. And thank you so much for Josh:

- Almost as soon as he heard, he hung up, left everything at work as it was, and came and got me. He then took me home, walked me in and then went back to work to pack up.

- I got in the bath to wash out the gravel and when he came back I got out. He then got me some antiseptic and an ice pack. Later he got me Nurofen and water.

- He then ordered a pizza and when he came back he'd also bought me Vanilla coke (which he doesn't like but knows I do) and a Toblerone!!

- He then tidied up the house, did the dishes and ironed his shirt.

I HAVE THE BEST HUSBAND IN THE WORLD!! Thank you so much for him.

CONNECT

It is so easy in life and in marriage to forget what has happened in the past. We tend to remember the bad and forget the good. Writing about these events can help create a catalogue of nice things he has done. Then every now and then you can read back over your journals and remind yourself of how much you love and appreciate your husband. These memories will increase your connection to your husband. I encourage you to also let these memories be a prompt to remind you to thank God for your husband and even more willingly do everything you can to bless him.

Make it fun

When I'd been married about 7 years I found this scrap of paper while I was cleaning out my filing cabinet. On it I had written my 'plan' for my marriage, before I got married:

> Make your marriage so good, so enjoyable, so satisfying that he has absolutely no desire/reason to look at another woman. Shouldn't be a nagging, pushy, bossy, demanding wife. Always make it fun.

I still agree with what I wrote all those years ago. This is absolutely what I want for my marriage. I certainly have not yet achieved this, but this is what I want. I want to be the kind of wife that my husband is happy to come home to, one whom my husband looks forward to spending time with on the weekends.

It's so strange how things change when you get married. Before you're married, you usually can't wait to see each other and spend time together...then 10 years later you see couples at a restaurant who can't think of a thing to say to each other. I think this happens because people get busy and lazy and because they become used to living with each other. They start to take each other for granted. Silly little arguments end up causing huge rifts.

The point I want to make here is that it's important to always have fun together. Don't make every day a stress. Don't hold onto grudges. Forgive quickly and create lots of opportunities to have fun together. They don't have to be expensive outings, you can have fun while washing the dishes or doing the gardening (true, it's a lot harder, but it can be done!). Joke and laugh together.

CONNECT

Earlier on in my marriage I used to get offended whenever Josh made a joke about me because I would read into it and interpret the joke as meaning that he didn't like me. I now realise I was being way too sensitive. Now I laugh at his jokes and poke fun at him right back. Laughing together is very important and our ability to do this now is one of my favourite things about our marriage. If your husband has fun with you, he's going to be a lot happier in the marriage, and so will you!

CONNECT

(not neglect)

IN SUMMARY:

Ask God to help you find interests in common

Give your husband's interests a genuine try

Put your husband's needs before your own

Forgive quickly—don't wait until your husband apologises

Apologise quickly, even if you're only 5% wrong

Keep arguments interesting, don't let them get nasty

Don't go to sleep angry with your husband

Make the most of the times when he wants to talk, even if it's inconvenient for you

Find out his best times for talking

Learn to really listen to what your husband is saying

Be clear with what you do and don't want—forget subtle hints

Don't keep secrets from him

Let him hang out with his mates and find some couple friends

Prioritise him before the kids

Honour your in-laws in your words and actions

Write down the nice things your husband does

Have fun in your marriage—don't make it a chore

HAVE SEX

(not reject)

1 Corinthians 7:2-5

But because there is so much sexual immorality, each man should have his own wife, and each woman should have her own husband.

The husband should fulfill his wife's sexual needs, and the wife should fulfill her husband's needs. The wife gives authority over her body to her husband, and the husband gives authority over his body to his wife.

Do not deprive each other of sexual relations, unless you both agree to refrain from sexual intimacy for a limited time so you can give yourselves more completely to prayer. Afterward, you should come together again so that Satan won't be able to tempt you because of your lack of self-control.

2 Timothy 2:22

Run from anything that stimulates youthful lusts. Instead, pursue righteous living, faithfulness, love, and peace. Enjoy the companionship of those who call on the Lord with pure hearts.

Introduction

The Bible is clear! God designed men and women to have sex with each other in marriage. He designed it to create intimacy, to connect a couple, to bring pleasure and to make babies. It is special because it's something a couple doesn't share with anyone else. It is the 'glue' that holds a marriage together.

Having regular, good, enjoyable, pleasurable sex is one of the best things you can do for your marriage.

Men don't usually need to be encouraged to have regular sex ☺.

But many, many wives have spoken with me about their sex life and nearly all of them have spoken about it as a problem. Either they enjoy having sex but are too busy to have it frequently or, more commonly, they don't enjoy sex at all.

This is a big concern as a good sex life is absolutely crucial to a great marriage. You can **accept** your husband, **respect** your husband and **connect** with your husband. But if you don't have good, regular sex with your husband you might as well just be friends. You are the only person he can have sex with!

Sex is such a significant need for men. If your husband is having regular, great, pleasurable sex it makes him confident, happy and peaceful. If he is being rejected by you (he will read it as rejection, whatever your reason for not having sex) he will be deflated, defeated and frustrated. And a deflated, defeated, frustrated man is not going to be very loving or attentive to your needs.

As a woman's need for sex is usually less than her husband's, she often doesn't realise how much it hurts him when she makes an excuse not to have sex. I once read a great analogy in a book[36]. It went something like this: Imagine you (the wife) have just received a phone call that you have won an all-expenses paid cruise around the world for two people. The minute your husband walks in the house you run up to him screaming in delight, "Guess what? Guess what? The most amazing thing has happened!" He barely looks at you and walks past you to go flop down onto the couch, murmuring, "Not now, I'm too tired." Imagine how deflated and frustrated you'd be! You have this amazing news that you want to share with your husband but he won't listen! The author (who was a male) said that this is exactly how a man feels when he approaches his wife for sex and she turns him down. He is so excited about spending time with her and wants to share the joy of making love with her—but she's just not interested.

If, for whatever reason, your sex life has ground to a halt, I encourage you to make it start happening again. This section will address some of the common challenges wives have with sex and some ways to improve your sex life so that you can **have sex** with your husband and not **reject** him.

36 I'm sorry —I have scoured my books to try to find the book in which I read this analogy, but I just can't find it. If any of my readers know which book it's from, please email me and I will add in the correct reference!

Make time for sex

In the movies two types of sexual activity tend to be portrayed: couples that have sex all the time and couples who have sex once a year on their wedding anniversary.

Most marriages probably fall somewhere in the middle. Sure, you read about people who have sex two or three times a day, but I think it's more likely to be the other extreme where tiredness, busyness and children mean it can be weeks between having sex. Dr Allan Meyer says, "Research indicates that nearly 50% of married women say that one of the biggest challenges they face with sexual intimacy is simply finding the energy for it"[37].

If this is you, that is, if you enjoy having sex but are just too busy or too tired to have it regularly, then I encourage you to ask God to help you understand and appreciate how important regular sex is to your husband. Also ask him to give you the desire to have great sex more often!

Then you need to start prioritising this time with your husband. We women make time to have showers, do our makeup and hair, and eat dinner. We make time to go clothes shopping, to go to a friend's party and to study. Sex with our husbands is just as important, in fact, more important, than these things! Make time for sex.

Try not to leave it until the end of the night when you are exhausted from the day. Why not have sex straight after dinner (pre-kids) or straight after the kids go to bed (post-kids)? Or think about your schedule and consider sex in the

---

37 *From Good Man to Valiant Man: Sexual Integrity in a Sex Crazy World,* Allan Meyer, 2008, Allan Meyer

HAVE SEX

morning or during a 'lunch date'. Get creative in finding time you can have alone and uninterrupted when you also have energy. If you're struggling to find time alone, ask God and your husband to give you ideas. Trust me, they will both give you suggestions[38]!

If you have a really busy lifestyle you might have to plan to have sex, otherwise it's just too easy to let day after day slip by, thinking, "I'm too tired tonight", "I have to get up early" or "I'm not feeling well". And before you know it, it's been a month. Even if you haven't noticed, I can assure you, your husband will have!

Planning is not something you should tell your husband about, it's just something you can sort out in your head. (For example, it's really unromantic to say, "Right hon, we have to have sex tonight. Right now. I have to get up early in the morning.") If you know you're going to be out late tomorrow night, make sure you have sex tonight. If you haven't had sex the last two nights, make sure you do tonight. If your husband is going away for a while, make sure you have as much sex as possible before he goes, and prioritise having sex as soon as possible once he returns.

What's the 'right' amount of sex? 1 Corinthians 7:3 says, "The husband should fulfill his wife's sexual needs, and the wife should fulfill her husband's needs." In other words, you should be seeking to have as much sex as your husband wants!

Most men (unless they're sick or really tired and rundown) would be happy to have sex every day. Unfortunately, most women don't have a sex drive to match. This is why it's

---

38 If you tell your husband that you're trying to find a good time for you to have sex when you're not too tired, he will move heaven and earth to make a time. He might even do the dishes for you or put the kids to bed!

important for a woman to make time for and prioritise sex. Aim to get to a point where sex is an everyday part of your married life together rather than a special event[39].

Please don't be disheartened if you're currently only having sex once a month. Start with small steps. Ask God to help you plan to have sex once a week. If you're having sex once a week, ask God to help you have it twice a week. If you're having sex twice a week, plan for three times. If you're having sex three times a week, plan for four times. If you're having sex four times a week...well, you get the picture[40]!

---

39 There are times when this just isn't possible, for example after surgery or after having a baby. Your husband will (hopefully) be very understanding in these times. Not being able to have intercourse does not mean you can't be loving and intimate with your husband though! It's important to resume regular sex as soon as possible once you are physically able. It may mean having sex less frequently initially, but work towards getting back to your previous frequency.
40 As couples get older, health issues may make frequent sex difficult. Perhaps the aim then should be quality, rather than quantity!

Increase your desire for sex

Sex is different for men and women.

Men usually have a strong sex drive, which is mainly physical. They will have an orgasm every time unless there is a physical or psychological issue. A man does not need to be emotionally connected to a woman to have sex with her.

Women usually have a fluctuating sex drive that is linked to the emotional connection she has with her husband. If a woman is not emotionally connected to her husband she probably won't want to have sex with him.

If you enjoy sex, but have a lower desire for sex than your husband, I encourage you to pray. Ask God to increase your desire for your husband, then begin to thank God for your husband. Thank God for all the good things your husband does for you and for all the things you love about him. This alone will help increase your desire! It may take time, but the more you do this, the more your desire will increase.

If you have little or no desire for sex at all, it's good to ask God to help you understand why. I've listed some of the most common reasons below, along with some suggestions for how to address them:

- **You're emotionally distant from your husband**

    This can become a vicious cycle. If you've stopped having sex with your husband because you're not emotionally connected to him, he will become less emotionally connected to you. This, in turn, will make him feel even further away and will further increase the gap between you. But if you start having sex again it will decrease the gap between you, making him more emotionally connected to you. Usually the more you have sex with him, the more he will begin to act in loving and considerate ways towards you.

- **You are angry or upset with your husband**

    If you are angry or upset with your husband you will probably have no desire for sex because sex is an emotional as well as a physical activity for you. You may also be tempted to withhold sex to punish him for the way he has treated you. If you're angry or upset with him I encourage you to go through the process for forgiving that I've outlined in *Forgive even if he doesn't say sorry*. Once God changes your heart, sex is a great way to 'do good' to your husband! It will help heal the relationship better than anything else[41].

- **You had sex before marriage**

    If you had sex before marriage (either with your husband or with someone else), sex can raise a whole range of negative emotions like guilt and insecurity. You may then carry these emotions throughout your marriage and wonder why you struggle to want sex. If this is you, I encourage you to repent. Ask God to forgive you for having sex outside of marriage. Ask Him to heal your broken sex drive and ask Him to give you a desire for your husband. Our God is an amazing, forgiving, healing God. He will forgive you and help you if you ask Him.

---

41 Of course, having sex is pointless if you are distant or annoyed the whole time. That is why it is important to forgive him first.

- **You have been sexually abused**

  It's absolutely horrific when girls are sexually abused. If that is you, I don't know what to say except to encourage you to go to God. He is able to heal the deepest of wounds. It may take time, but He can heal you (see Matthew 7:7-11). With God's help and healing you can come to a place of having a healthy view of and desire for sex with your husband. Some Christian counselling may also really help.

- **You have not yet learnt how to enjoy sex**

  While the act of sex can physically satisfy a man, he's only emotionally satisfied if his wife (who can be emotionally satisfied by the act of sex) is also physically satisfied. Your husband cares about whether or not you enjoy sex with him. He will enjoy sex so much more if you do too.

  Sex is incredibly natural, but so is eating and talking! Babies have to be taught how to feed themselves and how to talk. And married couples need to learn all they can about how to enjoy sex. Great sex does not just happen. It takes a lot of communication, practice and effort. That's the great thing about sex in marriage—you get lots of opportunities to practice! Learn together as a couple. Very few men are resistant to learning about sex. Your husband won't like it if you focus on all the things he is doing wrong, but if you ask him to read a book about sex, it's pretty safe to say he'll be keen.

  Intended for Pleasure: Sex Technique and Sexual Fulfilment in Christian Marriage by Ed Wheat M.D. and Gaye Wheat[42] is a great, practical book about how to have pleasurable sex. *The Act of Marriage: The Beauty*

---

42   *Intended for Pleasure: Sex Technique and Sexual Fulfilment in Christian Marriage*, 4th Edition, Ed & Gaye Wheat, 2010, Revell

of Sexual Love by Tim and Beverly LaHaye[43] is likewise very useful.

Both of these books make the point that husbands have a role in helping you enjoy sex, but so do you! Some simple strategies that can help you enjoy sex more are: be physically engaged in sex (don't just lie there—move!); communicate clearly, honestly and gently with your husband about what you do and don't enjoy; keep your mind focussed on your husband and your sexual experience; don't think about unrelated, mundane things; and make sure you're doing regular pelvic floor exercises[44]. There are many more strategies but these might give you a start. The next section will also give some suggestions for getting you in the right frame of mind.

Whatever your reason for not desiring sex, my best answer is to take your issue to God. Ask Him to forgive you, heal you and/or help you. He wants you to have a good, satisfying, enjoyable sex life with your husband and if you ask God to help you, He will!

---

43 *The Act of Marriage: The Beauty of Sexual Love*, Tim & Beverly LaHaye, 1976, Zondervan Publishing House
44 If you don't know what pelvic floor exercises are, look them up online. They are easy to do but hard to remember to do!

Sex should be fun

So, let's say you've made the time for sex and asked God to increase your desire. Now what? Below are some suggestions for you to make the most of every time you have sex:

It's all in the mind

Sex for women is all about their mind. Your husband can be touching your body in amazing ways but if you are thinking about what to make for dinner tomorrow night you are not going to have a great experience! Focus your thoughts on your husband and your current sexual experience, for example, think about:

- All the good things that you love about him
- How handsome and gorgeous he is
- How blessed you are to have such an amazing man wanting you!
- What he is doing to you, right now
- What you'd love him to be doing to you next
- What you can do to excite him
- How he is making you feel

You should **not** be thinking about:

- The things that annoy you about him
- The work you need to do tomorrow
- Another man (more on this soon)

Start thinking about sex at the start of the day. Start thinking about when you'll have sex, what you'll wear and what you'd like to do to your husband. Even better, text him[45] and tell him exactly what you're planning. Then both of you will be looking forward to the evening with great anticipation!

Take the initiative

Take the initiative. Don't make him ask if you're willing to have sex (especially if he is used to you rejecting him), just start kissing him and touching him. He'll get the picture very quickly.

Get in the mood

If you find it hard to feel sexy after doing dishes, hanging out washing and putting kids to bed, do some practical things to get yourself in the mood. Have a shower or bath, put on some nice lingerie[46], turn on some mood music and light some candles. As you're getting ready, start getting your mind ready too, thinking good and sexy thoughts about your husband.

Have fun

Make sex fun! However:

- Only do things that both of you are comfortable doing. If your husband wants to do something you don't love the idea of, talk with him about it and pray about it. If it's

---

45 Only if you know no-one will see his phone!

46 If you don't have the money to spend on fancy lingerie (although this seems to be an expense most husbands will find the money for) you can get really nice sets for very little money from shops like Kmart, Big W and Target. They may not be the best quality, but seriously, they're only going to stay on you for a few minutes. It's the look you're going for here, not longevity!

not something wrong, maybe ask God to help you get comfortable with it.

- Sex should only ever involve the two of you. It shouldn't include looking at other people (e.g. pornography).

- Be careful about doing anything that could take the place of your spouse. This includes sex toys that could take the place of your husband (for example a vibrator which could emasculate your husband by telling him a machine can do the job better than him!). God has designed sexual fulfilment to come from a husband and wife working together to give each other pleasure.

Apart from those three restrictions, have fun! Try different things to excite and enjoy each other. Try different rooms, different positions, different roles, different outfits—keep it interesting! The more fun sex is, the more your desire will increase.

Don't fret about having an orgasm

Don't worry about having an orgasm every time you have sex—studies have shown that most women don't. Usually a whole range of factors need to be in place for women to orgasm. Instead, keep your focus on enjoying the sexual intimacy with your husband. Then, even if you don't orgasm, you can enjoy the experience and the fact that your husband desires you and wants you. You are far more likely to orgasm if you are not worrying about whether you will or not!

Focus on intimacy

Keep in mind that even though men are more physical when it comes to sex, intimacy is still very important to them.

In his article on sex drive[47], Richard Sine quotes Esther Perel, a couples and family therapist from New York City:

> *"That doesn't mean men don't seek intimacy, love, and connection in a relationship, just as women do. They just view the role of sex differently. 'Women want to talk first, connect first, then have sex,' Perel explains. 'For men, sex is the connection. Sex is the language men use to express their tender loving vulnerable side,' Perel says. 'It is their language of intimacy.'"*

Perel makes an excellent point. Sex is one of the main methods husbands use to connect with their wives. Your husband is not just an unthinking animal, desperately seeking physical pleasure, seeing you as a piece of meat, uncaring as to how involved you are. Yes, your husband really wants to have sex. But even more than that, he really wants to have an intimate, loving, passionate, exciting sexual experience *with you*. The way he opens up to you and says loving things during sex is him showing his real self, not him just trying to 'butter you up'. Clinical, routine sex will not satisfy his need for intimacy.

All hail the quickie

You don't have to have a long, sensual love making session every time you have sex. It's great to have these regularly, but a 'quickie' when you are busy is better than nothing!

47 *Sex Drive: How Do Men and Women Compare?*, Richard Sine, 22 August 2013, retrieved from http://www.webmd.com/sex/features/sex-drive-how-do-men-women-compare

Men are very visual

Before Josh met me he used to joke about the kind of woman he wanted to marry: "Must shave legs, must shave underarms, must not shave face."

Even though he was joking, he was actually very serious. He wanted to marry a woman who would look after herself and would make an effort with the way she looked. He's not alone—men are very visual and it's important for them to be physically attracted to their wives.

This area is a constant challenge for me. I'm not one of those people who find things like makeup, hair styles and fashion easy. I certainly tried a lot harder when I was going out with Josh but soon after getting married I got lazy. I stopped exercising (it is very difficult to maintain routine when you first get married) and I stopped wearing makeup because I'd moved to Darwin where the constant hot weather made makeup just slide off my face. I had some very bad haircuts and colours, and I didn't feel all that great about how I looked. Instead of doing something about it, I told myself it didn't really matter how I looked anyway.

One day Josh made a passing comment. I can't remember specifically what he said, but it included the word 'daggy'. I was hurt, but I knew he was right. I'd been having days at work when I would look at my hair in the bathroom and just feel depressed at how bad I looked. I'd run into people while shopping and feel self-conscious.

Paul says in 1 Timothy:

And I want women to be modest in their appearance. They should wear decent and appropriate clothing and not draw attention to themselves by the way they fix their hair or by wearing gold or pearls or expensive clothes. For women who claim to be devoted to God should make themselves attractive by the good things they do.

1 Timothy 2:9-10

So many women spend far too much time worrying about how they look on the outside instead of focussing on how they 'look' on the inside. Instead, we should be focussing on loving God and others—this is what makes us truly beautiful.

However, I don't believe that this means we shouldn't care about how we look. We should want to make ourselves attractive—not to impress other women or to make us feel good about ourselves, but to continue to attract our husbands. We want them to desire us and want us, not be repulsed by us!

So, after Josh made that comment I made myself a rule that I wouldn't go out unless I had make up on, was dressed appropriately and my hair was done. I would always wear make up to work and try to buy clothes that were attractive, fashionable and modest. I think this will always be an area that I will have to work on because it doesn't come easily to me. And it's impossible to always be well presented, especially when I'm cleaning! But when I do dress up and wear something nice, I feel good and can be confident that my husband won't be embarrassed by my appearance. Taking the time (not ridiculous amounts of time, though!) to wear nice clothes, wear makeup, get good haircuts and colours, shave or wax, and paint your nails is worth it. *He's* worth it!

Affairs can be avoided

Hebrews 13:4 says, "Give honour to marriage, and remain faithful to one another in marriage. God will surely judge people who are immoral and those who commit adultery."

Faithfulness in marriage is really important to me. Hopefully it is to you too! Affairs destroy a marriage like no other sin. I think Jesus allowed for divorce when there was unfaithfulness[48] because unfaithfulness is literally taking two people who have become one flesh[49] and tearing them apart. A marriage that has been torn apart this way is difficult to repair.

I want to explain what faithfulness means, why people are unfaithful and how to avoid being unfaithful.

In the Ten Commandments we are taught not to commit adultery[50]. This is pretty clear: don't touch someone you're not married to inappropriately, don't kiss them, don't have sex with them. But Jesus took it one step further as you can see in the passage below:

> You have heard the commandment that says, "You must not commit adultery." But I say, anyone who even looks at a woman with lust has already committed adultery with her in her heart.
> **Matthew 5:27-28**

---

48 See Matthew 19:9.
49 See Genesis 2:24, Mark 10:8 and Ephesians 5:31.
50 See Exodus 20:14.

Jesus taught that if we want to be faithful, we need to be faithful not just in our actions but in our thoughts. Even desiring to be with someone else is a sin.

Before I got married I could never understand how a Christian (who loved God, read the Bible, prayed, went to church and so on) could be unfaithful. And let's face it—there's a lot of Christians who have been unfaithful. People who've been Christians for a long time. People who are leaders in a church. Even pastors.

I was pretty judgemental towards people who were unfaithful. I think that was partly because I assumed that because I was a 'good' Christian it was something I never could or would do.

Then one day soon after getting married I remember seeing a cute guy at the bus stop. I checked him out and started thinking about him, when suddenly I remembered with shock that I was married and that what I was doing was bordering on cheating! I had been so used to doing this when I was single (when it was normal and okay—within reason!) that I had just 'naturally' done it without thinking.

Just as I did, it's easy to think: "I would never cheat", but the truth is, no matter how strong you are, or how long you've been a Christian, or how well you were brought up, **YOU ARE VERY CAPABLE OF HAVING AN AFFAIR**[51] and chances are you will be tempted to do so more than once in your married life. It is so important that you realise this, otherwise you probably won't take the rest of this section seriously. The Bible makes it clear that we shouldn't think we're immune to temptation.

---

51 I dislike the use of capitals unless absolutely necessary. Clearly, I think it's absolutely necessary in this case!

If you think you are standing strong, be careful not to fall. The temptations in your life are no different from what others experience.
1 Corinthians 10:12-13a

I discovered this when some Christian friends of mine started walking down the pathway of being unfaithful. Also, around this time a leader at my church lent me some books on marriage. One of them, *Lonely Husbands, Lonely Wives* by Dennis Rainey[52], helped me understand for the first time how good Christian people could be unfaithful.

What I realised is that unfaithfulness is rarely a random one-night stand with a total stranger. I have become convinced that unfaithfulness usually requires a combination of factors that build up. I'm sure there are more but I believe these are the main three factors:

1. Increasing *distance* between you and your husband

2. Increasing *distance* between you and God

3. Increasing *closeness* between you and another man

Let me explain these further:

1. Increasing distance between you and your husband

- You are not spending quality time with each other, due to sickness, busyness, tiredness and/or having children.

- You're not feeling loved and he's not feeling respected.

- You're arguing more.

- You're frustrated and disappointed with each other.

52 *Lonely Husbands, Lonely Wives*, Dennis Rainey, 1989, Word Incorporated

- You're feeling lonely.
- You're not having a lot of sex.

2. **Increasing distance between you and God**
   - You're not reading your Bible and praying.
   - You're not spending time with God.
   - You're not attending church as frequently, or if you do, you're just going through the motions.

3. **Increasing closeness between you and another man**
   - You start to become friends with another man. He may be a work colleague, a member of the same ministry team at church, someone from your sporting team or a friend of your husband. This friendship is probably very innocent, platonic and not sought out.

   - For some reason you 'connect' with this man. Perhaps you're physically attracted to him but this is not usually the primary reason. You probably connect with him because you have an interest in common that your husband does not share.

   - This man becomes closer. He really listens to you. He laughs at your jokes. He respects and admires you. He is interested in understanding how you tick. He seems to appreciate things about you that your spouse doesn't even notice.

   - You start thinking about this man more and more.

   - You start telling him things you don't even tell your husband.

   - You start really looking forward to spending time with him, even more than you do with your husband.

- You start thinking that life would have been so much better if you'd married him instead.

As Dennis Rainey explained, at this point you've probably done nothing physical, but you've already been unfaithful: you're having an emotional affair. And an emotional affair is just a short step away from a physical affair. That is because our thoughts lead to desires which lead to action[53]. Even if it never becomes a physical affair an emotional affair can still be devastating to a marriage. It undermines trust and can cause a great chasm between you and your husband. As Jesus said in Matthew 5:27-28, it's not just about our actions but about our thoughts—even desiring to be with someone else is a sin.

When I understood the steps that are usually taken to have an affair, I got really scared. I got scared because I realised that I could very easily do that! I realised that if I wasn't careful I could casually walk down the pathway of being unfaithful without even being aware of where I was headed. I love meeting new people and making friends, and at the time had quite a few male friends. I thought because I wasn't attracted to them physically it wasn't a problem. But although there was *technically* nothing wrong with me having male friends, it was dangerous to put myself in that position. By becoming friends with a man I was opening myself up to the possibility of becoming emotionally attached.

Once I understood that I needed to be wary of having emotional affairs as well as physical affairs, I started looking at how I could make sure I remained faithful.

---

53 See James 1:14-15.

Really, it's about doing the opposite of the things that lead to unfaithfulness:

1. Increase the *closeness* between you and your husband
2. Increase the *closeness* between you and God
3. Increase the *distance* between you and other men

Again, I'll explain these further:

1. Increase the closeness between you and your husband

If you accept your husband, respect your husband, connect with your husband and have great, regular sex with your husband, you will increase the closeness between you.

It also helps to remove any external influences that give you a negative view of your marriage by presenting an unrealistic ideal (such as some romance novels and movies).

2. Increase the closeness between you and God

Prioritise praying, reading the Bible, worshipping God and spending time with other Christians. The more you are loving God and knowing Him the more you will want to do what is pleasing to Him and the easier it will be to love your husband.

3. Increase the distance between you and other men

The Bible says:

> Run from anything that stimulates youthful lusts. Instead, pursue righteous living, faithfulness, love, and peace. Enjoy the companionship of those who call on the Lord with pure hearts.
>
> **2 Timothy 2:22**

We need to run away from anyone that stimulates our lust! This is hard to do once you're already in an emotional affair with someone[54]. So the challenge is to put that distance in place before you get emotionally attached to someone. One really effective way to do this is to give yourself boundaries.

I use the term 'boundaries' to describe self-imposed rules that will act like a warning when you are going into dangerous territory.

For example: Let's say eating a whole block of chocolate is wrong. If this is the case, it's no good saying to yourself, "Don't eat the whole block". This is because you could then eat all but the last piece and still not have done anything 'wrong'...and chances are you will end up thinking you might as well just go ahead and finish it! Instead, consider where the 'wrong' really starts, for example, half a block, then set the boundary way back, for example, one row. Then if you eat one row, get tempted and end up eating two rows, you will feel guilty and stop. But you still haven't actually done anything wrong!

It's the same with helping yourself be faithful. There is no point having a rule for yourself of "Don't sleep with someone else". By the time you're in a fully-fledged emotional affair it will be hard to stop. Instead, it's far better to put boundaries in place so you can prevent yourself from even *starting* an emotional affair.

54 If you're in this place, you need to repent and then end it immediately. You need to cease all communication straight away. Ask God to give you wisdom if you should tell the man why you are ending the friendship (He may genuinely see it just as a friendship. Unlikely, but possible.) or if you should just ignore any attempts he makes at future contact. Also ask God to give you wisdom how to tell your husband (see *Let your actions build trust*). Confess to him as soon as possible and ask his forgiveness.

Here are the boundaries that I have chosen for myself for my interactions with other men (not including family, obviously!):

- **Don't seek out friendships with other men**

  I can be friendly with other men, but not friends with them exclusive of Josh. If I find I'm even starting to emotionally connect with a particular man, I do all I can to disconnect with him. This would include things such as not deliberately going to talk to him and only spending time with him in the context of a group. I tone down my friendliness. Of course I can still be polite and nice, but I avoid anything that could be construed as being flirtatious.

- **Don't contact other men**

  Where I can possibly avoid it I don't ring, email, text, write to or send Facebook messages to a man. There may be times when I need to do so for a genuine reason but it is always for a purpose, not just to chat.

- **Avoid spending lots of time with other men**

  Where possible I avoid being part of a team or project where it will require me to spend a lot of time by myself with just one other male. If this is a requirement of my work I pray and ask God to help me get out of that situation[55].

---

55 Once I was faced with this situation. There was a guy in another department at my work who I found easy to talk to and joke with. I didn't see him very often, but then a project came up where we were both on the same large team. The team then had to split up into pairs to complete certain parts of the project. I was in charge of allocating the pairs and it was tempting to pair up with this man as I knew we'd work well together. Thankfully, I had recently put these boundaries in place so I deliberately put him with someone else. Not long after this he started getting a bit flirty with me. I was so grateful that I was not working with him! It made it very easy to ignore his flirtation and start avoiding him. After getting a few cold responses from me he soon got the message.

- **Don't be alone with another man, where possible**

   Where reasonably possible, I avoid car trips alone with a man. Of course, there are times where it cannot be avoided because it would be impractical to make other arrangements, but this should be the exception, not the rule. If I do have to be alone with another man, such as on a car trip, I restrict conversation to general topics, not personal topics[56].

   I also avoid being alone in a house with a man. If for some reason I am put in the position of a man coming to my house when no-one else is around, I go outside the front of my house and talk to them there. (Tradies are an exception of course, although I still do not stay around and chat with them.)

- **Avoid touching another man, except in appropriate circumstances**

   I try to avoid touching other men, unless it is appropriate to the situation (such as hugging a man goodbye who is moving interstate). I find this very difficult because, with physical touch being my love language, it's natural for me to touch people on the arm or shoulder to show that I care. However, I am aware that this can be misinterpreted very easily.

All of my boundaries mean that I will not have the *opportunity* to build a friendship with a man that could turn

---

56 This might seem a little over the top, but think about it: a car is actually a very intimate, private space. There's no-one else to talk to and no-one can hear what you say. On the times I have had to go on a trip with another man I have found it very awkward. They have your undivided attention and vice-versa. You feel compelled to make conversation. On one-off trips it's not too bad, but if you regularly make a car trip with the same man you will actually have a lot of time for private conversation, and this can lead to building an emotional connection.

into an emotional affair nor will I have the *opportunity* to have a physical relationship with another man as I will only ever be with other men in a public place.

It also means I'll avoid the "appearance of evil"[57]. If I was to regularly spend time with a man or if a man was coming into my home when Josh was not there, other people may suspect or assume that I was having an affair. Even if the relationship was innocent, I would be throwing doubt onto the integrity of my marriage. This is disrespectful to my husband. Also, it will weaken my witness to others if they think I am doing the wrong thing.

I have found my boundaries to be very effective. If I start to connect with a guy or am alone with him all my 'warning bells' go off. I feel uncomfortable and quickly try to change the situation. At this stage I haven't done anything even close to wrong but the boundaries make me aware of potential danger, enabling me to change my behaviour so I can protect myself and protect my marriage.

My boundaries are not there to make my life difficult but to help me from developing both emotional and physical affairs. I have chosen these boundaries, so I don't find them cumbersome or limiting. They might seem over the top to other people but I don't want to do anything that could jeopardize my relationship with Josh. I would rather be too careful than be too complacent and lose my husband. My marriage is completely worth it. And if you know someone whose spouse has been unfaithful you'll probably agree with me that my boundaries are not extreme.

I'm not suggesting that you have to adopt my personal boundaries, I am just sharing what has helped me. I encourage you to pray and ask God what your personal

---

57 See 1 Thessalonians 5:22.

boundaries should be. They may be different from mine, which is fine—the purpose of them is to not to be a huge burden but to give you protection. Your boundaries may well save your marriage!

Don't look or touch

A common saying is "Look, but don't touch". I don't agree with this at all. As I mentioned earlier, the Bible teaches that you should "Run from anything that stimulates youthful lusts."[58] You shouldn't even look.

Take chocolate for example (or any other food that you find particularly tempting). Even if you're a real chocoholic, you probably don't think about it 24/7. But if someone talks about it, or puts chocolate in front of you, you'll probably eat it. Now, if you've decided that you shouldn't eat chocolate because you're trying to be healthy, standing around looking at an open box of chocolates isn't going to help you avoid temptation. Instead, it would be much easier if you remove the chocolates from view and surround yourself with healthy food.

The same goes with other men. Looking at them, thinking about them or talking about them is only going to create temptation for you. Martin Luther is credited with saying, "You cannot keep birds from flying over your head but you can keep them from building a nest in your hair". We can't control who walks past us in the street but we can stop ourselves from taking a second look and then thinking about them!

If I see a good looking man, my policy is never to double-take. Never to look back. Never to deliberately look. Instead I try to spend as much time as I can with my husband (the healthy food!). It is much easier to avoid temptation than to resist it.

---

58 See 2 Timothy 2:22.

The same goes for any pictures you might see of good looking men on the internet, or actors you see in TV shows or movies. If you find that you are looking at them in any way that might be lustful, you need to stop looking! This might mean giving up on a TV show if you're not going to be able to think innocent, pure thoughts while watching it[59].

It might sound extreme, but I think that is what the Bible means when it says to **run** from anything that stimulates youthful lusts. Besides, think about how you'd feel if you caught your husband ogling some beautiful woman. We don't want our husbands looking lustfully at other women so we shouldn't look lustfully at other men.

---

59 A great Scripture for this situation is Philippians 4:8b *"Fix your thoughts on what is true, and honourable, and right, and pure, and lovely, and admirable. Think about things that are excellent and worthy of praise."* If something you are looking at is making you think about something that is not honourable, right and pure, then it is not good for you. Instead start focusing on your husband and all the great things about him!

HAVE SEX

(not reject)

IN SUMMARY:

Ask God to help you make the time to have sex more often

Ask God to increase your desire for sex

Get your head in the right space for sex, take the initiative and have fun

Do your best to look attractive for your husband

Choose boundaries for yourself that will help you avoid an affair

Don't look at other men—enjoy looking at your husband instead

Recommended reading

I've referred to a lot of great relationship and marriage books throughout this book. All of them are worth reading.

But there are four books that I think *every* wife should buy and read. They are brilliant. They will change the way you look at your husband for the better. I recommend them all the time and hear excellent feedback from people who read them. These four books are:

1. *The Five Love Languages* by Dr Gary Chapman
2. *Personality Plus* by Florence Littauer
3. *Love & Respect* by Dr Emerson Eggerichs
4. *His Needs, Her Needs* by Willard F. Harley

They are all best sellers (because they are great books!) and can therefore be bought quite easily and cheaply. They are well worth the investment of your money and time.

If you want your marriage to be great, please read them!

Conclusion

I realise that this whole book is very counter-cultural. Unlike most books, I'm not advocating a 50/50, 'meet half way' or a compromise approach. I'm not showing you how to do something for your husband in order to get him to do something for you. Instead, my motto is taken from the pastors who did our pre-marriage counselling: "Expect nothing, give everything"[60]. I believe that we should give to our husbands, expecting nothing in return.

I speak to so many women who are completely against this idea. They say: "Sure, I realise that I need to make an effort, but so does he! If he's not putting any effort in, why should I? Why should I be the one to make all the sacrifices? Why should I be nice to him when he never does anything for me? We should be compromising! We should take it in turns to get what we want!"

The problem with this way of thinking is that it doesn't solve the problem of how to have a good marriage. If you really want to have a good marriage, a great marriage, a marriage that is satisfying and enjoyable and fun and long lasting...the kind of marriage every girl dreams of (I'm sure it's safe to say no-one dreams of a marriage full of frustration, arguments, bitterness and loneliness), then *you* can do something about it.

It's all about changing your perspective. You have a choice as to what kind of marriage you have. You can be a wife who nags, complains and whinges about her terrible marriage (and trust me, it *will* be a terrible marriage if you do that) or you can be a woman who makes it her personal mission to be the best

---

60 Thanks Con & Annette Keros!

wife she can be. A good marriage takes at least one person being a good spouse, and it might as well be you. Because if you sit around waiting for your husband to suddenly figure it all out and become the world's greatest husband you might be waiting a very, very long time. An amazing marriage doesn't just happen. It is something you have to choose on a daily basis.

Of course your husband should do his bit too. He should be loving, caring and considerate. He should lay down his life for you as Christ laid down his life for the church. He should listen to you, honour you and consider himself incredibly blessed to have you as his wife. He should make being a good husband a priority and goal in his life. He should ask you what he can change to make you happier. He should be grateful for every loving, respectful, kind thing you do.

He definitely should. It should not be one sided. It should not be left to you to work at the marriage. You shouldn't have to give to him time and time again only for him to do nothing. It's not fair for to you do everything right while he just reaps the rewards without having to lift a finger. He should be putting in as much effort as you.

And if I had written a book for husbands I would have lots of advice about how he can be a good husband, irrespective of what his wife was doing.

But because most men aren't interested in reading marriage books I've written this just for wives. My heart is to help you realise that you have the power to improve your marriage even if your husband isn't interested in changing.

I believe that if you take a huge step of faith and ask God to help you meet your husband's needs, God will slowly, eventually work on your husband too. Your husband probably won't change as fast as you would like. And he'll never be perfect.

But I believe that God honours our faithfulness. Of course, I can't promise that your husband will change, but if you put your trust in God and do all you can to meet your husband's needs, then even if your husband chooses to walk away from your marriage, you can have the peace of knowing you did all you could.

Whether your marriage is currently bad or good, hopefully your heart is for it to continually get better. If you want to improve your marriage, ask God to help you to understand and meet your husband's four main needs, which are for you to:

1. **Accept** him
2. **Respect** him
3. **Connect** with him
4. **Have sex** with him

I encourage you to ask your husband if this is true—if this is what he really needs from you. And if he says yes, pray and ask God to help you meet these four needs!

If you need help remembering the four main needs, the best I can do is rearrange the letters of the key words to give you... drum roll please...CARS. Yep, CARS. CARS help you move forward at a fast speed, don't they? And when you drive cars you can reach a destination, right? Cars, cars, cars, cars, cars, cars. Connect, Accept, Respect, Sex. Okay, so it's not the world's most meaningful acronym, but hopefully it will still help you remember!

On a more serious note, please don't be too hard on yourself and think: "I can't do this! I'll never do all that. What's the point of even trying? It's just another list for me to fail against." Instead, I hope you can see this as a positive challenge—you have the power to make your marriage so much better. You can do this by asking God to forgive you for where you've gone wrong in the past and then asking Him to help you accept, respect, connect and have sex with your husband. If you ask God for His help, He will help you! You will probably have to ask God for help every day but the more you do it, the easier it will get.

I wish I could say that I happily and successfully meet all four of Josh's greatest needs all the time but that simply isn't true. I still struggle to do so. I have found, however, that after 18 years of marriage it is much easier than it was in the beginning! I am so much more relaxed in my marriage and enjoy it so much more, thanks to God's continual help, guidance and encouragement. I love my husband and my marriage. I am so blessed. Not just because I have a wonderful husband, but because God was kind enough to show me as a newlywed where I was going wrong and to gently steer me towards the right direction.

I pray that this book has given you some helpful practical advice. I pray that God will use it to bless, encourage and challenge you. Most of all I pray you will realise that you have the power to make your marriage amazing. That power is God enabling you to stop correcting, directing, neglecting and rejecting your husband, and instead enabling you to accept, respect, connect and have lots and lots of lovely sex with your husband ☺.

Thanks for reading!

Sally

A WISE WOMAN BUILDS HER HOME,
BUT A FOOLISH WOMAN TEARS IT DOWN
WITH HER OWN HANDS.

Proverbs 14:1

A WISE WOMAN BUILDS HER HOME,
BUT A FOOLISH WOMAN TEARS IT DOWN
WITH HER OWN HANDS.

Proverbs 14:1

Acknowledgements

Thank you so much to my mum, the amazing Jenny Furniss. All my life you have modelled what it means to be a great wife and have been such an inspiration to me with your love for God and for Dad. Thank you for your many edits and recommendations for this book, as well as your continual encouragement and support.

Thank you to my beautiful sister, Rebekah Rodda, not only for your insightful and helpful edits, but also for your persistence in motivating me to get this book finished. I don't think it would ever have been published without your regular advice and suggestions. Everyone should have a mum and a sister like you two! I love you both so much.

Thank you to Dr Barry Chant, Dr Allan Meyer, Dr Vanessa Chant, Pastor Bill Vasilakis, Pastor Robyn Bettcher and Pastor Sally-Anne Rainbow. You are all very wise, very experienced and very busy people. Thank you for taking the time to read my book and give me such valuable and insightful feedback.

Thank you also to all my friends who have patiently listened as I've given you advice (whether you've liked it or not) and a huge thanks to those of you who have read my drafts, suggested titles or acted as a sounding board: Hayley Heath, Rin Montroy, Sarah Strack, Jackie Poyzer, Mark Furniss, David Furniss, Alex Hall, Linda Smith and Vanessa Dolphin.

Finally, thank you to Josh. Thank you for allowing me to share so openly about our lives, for supporting me throughout the long process of writing this book and for being the best of all best friends. I love you so much.

About the author

Sally Poyzer is a credentialed pastor with CRC Churches International and has spent many years ministering to women, particularly in the area of marriage. She is passionate about sharing how God can help wives enjoy being married.

With a background in corporate training and a Bachelor in Adult and Vocational Education, Sally is an experienced and enthusiastic preacher and teacher. She has her own consulting business, specialising in writing and facilitating customised training programs, as well as writing and formatting a range of organisational documents.

Sally was married at nineteen to Josh Poyzer, who is now the Senior Pastor of Portlife Church. They have been married for over eighteen years and live with their two gorgeous children, Promise and Rockford, in Adelaide, South Australia.

Get in touch

If you have any comments or questions about this book, or if you would like to invite Sally to speak at your church or conference, you can send her a message via her Facebook page www.facebook.com/sallypoyzerauthor or her website, www.sallypoyzer.com.au. She would love to hear from you!

If this book has been a blessing to you, please help spread the word by reviewing it on www.goodreads.com, www.amazon.com and by sharing Sally's website with your friends.

CPSIA information can be obtained
at www.ICGtesting.com
Printed in the USA
BVOW06s2154290317
479821BV00011B/78/P